WHOLENESS OF FAITH AND LIFE

WHOLENESS OF FAITH AND LIFE:
ORTHODOX CHRISTIAN ETHICS

Part One
Patristic Ethics

Part Two
Church Life Ethics

Part Three
Orthodox Social Ethics

Stanley S. Harakas

WHOLENESS OF FAITH AND LIFE:
ORTHODOX CHRISTIAN ETHICS

Part Two

Church Life Ethics

HOLY CROSS ORTHODOX PRESS
Brookline, Massachusetts

© Copyright 1999 Holy Cross Orthodox Press
Published by Holy Cross Orthodox Press
50 Goddard Avenue
Brookline, Massachusetts 02445

Part Two - ISBN 1-885652-29-1

On the cover: Detail from *Transfiguration*, 1547 from *To Dodekaorto* of the Dionysiou Monastery of Mt. Athos, Greece. With thanks to Fr. Petros, Abbot.

Library of Congress Cataloging–in–Publication Data
Harakas, Stanley S.
  Wholeness of Faith and Life / Stanley S. Harakas.
    p.   cm.
  Includes bibliographical references.
  Contents: Pt. 1 Patristic ethics
  ISBN 1-885652-26-7 (pbk.)
  1. Christian ethics—Orthodox Eastern authors. I. Title.
BJ250.H375   1999
241'.0419—dc21   98-56047
                                                CIP

Table of Contents

To the Trinitarian God,
Who calls us to partake of the solid food of Faith, which
"is for the mature, for those who have their faculties trained
by practice to distinguish good from evil" (Hebrews 5:14).

And to
Lukas DeFilippo, our Beloved Grandson

INTRODUCTION

Upon my retirement after 29 years of teaching Orthodox Christian Ethics at Holy Cross Greek Orthodox School of Theology in 1995, I carried with me six incomplete manuscripts, started at different times over the years, but not brought to completion and publication.

The first of these was published a year later under the title *Of Life and Salvation: Reflections on Living the Christian Life (Based on the Fourteen Scripture Readings of the Orthodox Christian Church's Sacrament of Holy Unction)* (Minneapolis: Light and Life Publishing Co., 1996). In God's providence opportunities for reflection and writing came to me during the first three years of retirement that contributed to one of the remaining publication projects I brought into retirement from Brookline, MA: a collection of some articles written over the years in the field of Orthodox Christian Ethics. A number of these writings were in journals and other publications not readily available. Thus, this second fruit of my retirement came into being.

Wholeness of Faith and Life is a compilation of sixteen essays on themes that seek to explicate various aspects of Orthodox Christian Ethics. Of these, six are being published here for the first time. Even though they have been written over a long period of time, these chapters have been selected with an eye to their coherence in viewpoint and perspective. This coherence has led to their being published in three parts: Part 1 – Patristic Ethics; Part 2 – Church Life Ethics; Part 3 – Orthodox Social ethics. Underlying that unity of theme are several fundamental perspectives that flow from the Orthodox Christian Ethics.

The first of these is the consistent view that Orthodox Christian ethical teaching and stances are derivative of the Orthodox

Christian theological worldview. For Eastern Orthodox Christianity, understood as a continuous theological stance approaching the beginning of its third millenium next year, there is no autonomous ethic.

The second fundamental perspective pervading each of the studies in this volume is the sense of the inter-relatedness and wholeness of all aspects of the Christian life. Thus, "wholistic" is a term that permeates this volume. Faith, knowledge, ethics, life, ethos, intents, motives, consequences, norms, overt behavior, and inner dispositions are part of a single fabric. There are no "ethical reductionisms" in this ethical perspective.

This book cannot be understood as a comprehensive ethical treatise. It does however, have unity. In the first part, "Patristic Ethics" the roots of contemporary Orthodox Christian reflection are examined in six essays that explicate aspects of the biblico-patristic heritage of the Eastern Orthodox Christian ethical tradition. Most of the topics discussed and developed in this part of the volume deal with issues of personal ethics.

The second part of the book, consisting of five essays, deals with a broadly conceived "Ecclesial Ethic," seeking to deal with the ethical self-understanding of the Orthodox Church, including its inner relationships as well as the Church's own orientation to "that which is not Church."

The last five chapters make up the final part of this volume, which consciously faces outward in dealing with issues of the social and economic context in which the Church lives, and toward which the Church's ethic assumes a certain responsibility. This part is called "Orthodox Social Ethics." It addresses political, social, and economic issues of interest to responsible citizens from an Eastern Orthodox perspective.

Thus, selected areas of personal, ecclesial, and social ethics from the life and thought of the Eastern Orthodox Christian tradition are examined in this volume, providing the reader with an insight to some aspects of the way the Orthodox Church reflects and opines ethically. The reader will quickly discern that no effort has been made to eliminate the concrete historical occasions in which these offerings were made. Though they bear the marks of their conference and meeting origins, I believe that they are capable of standing as authentic expressions of Orthodox Christian Ethics over the long run.

This volume could not have come into being without the numerous invitations to participate in conferences and meetings, with assigned topics for presentation. Special thanks to the Ecumenical Patriarchate, the World Council of Churches, other Orthodox and ecumenical agencies and especially the Board of Trustees, the Administration, the Faculty and Students of Holy Cross Greek Orthodox School of Theology who formed the context over the years for these reflections and studies. In particular, I thank Dr. Anton Vrame, Managing Editor of Holy Cross Orthodox Press, for his support and encouragement in bringing this three-part book to fruition. It was he and the Editorial Board of the Holy Cross Orthodox Press that decided to publish the manuscript in three separate and handy volumes.

Permissions to republish nine articles have been received (in order of appearance in the volume) from *The Greek Orthodox Theological Review* ("Ethical Teaching in St. Gregory Theologian's Writings") *Ex Auditu* ("Resurrection and Ethics in St. John Chrysostom"), *The Greek Orthodox Theological Review* ("Ethical Teachings in the Canons of the Penthekte Council"), the Patriarchal Centre in Geneva ("The Teaching of Peace in the Fathers"), *Orthodoxes Forum* of Munich, Germany (Icon and Ethics), the Edwin Mellen Press ("Responding to Contemporary Challenges to Orthodoxy"), the Society of Christian Ethics ("A Case Study in Eastern Orthodox Ethics on Rich and Poor"), the World Council of Churches ("An Orthodox Ethic of Development"), *St. Vladimir's Theological Quarterly* ("The Integrity of Creation") and *The Journal of Medicine and Philosophy* ("An Eastern Orthodox Approach to Bioethics").

Gratitude is also expressed to those who invited me to speak on different topics at conferences and meetings, including the School of Theology of the University of Thessalonke, Greece, Barry University in Miami, FL, and the American Academy of

Religion. The occasions of these six presentations are referred to in the notes for each chapter. The six previously unpublished essays are: "Presuppositions for Ethical Method in St. Gregory the Theologian's *Theological Orations,*" "Ethical Decision-Making in St. Basil's Long Rules" (Presidential Address – American Theological Society), "The Doctrine of the Trinity in Eastern Orthodox Ethics," "Eastern Orthodox Community Ethics," "European Multiformity and Dimensions of Orthodox Christian Social Ethics," and "Religion in the Public Square: An Orthodox Reflection on the First Amendment."

Spring Hill, Florida
Feast of St. Anastasia (+304)
December 22, 1998

Introduction to Part Two:

Church Life Ethics

Part Two of this book is titled "Church Life Ethics." The contents have a trajectory that moves from Faith (Chapter 7, "The Doctrine of the Trinity in Eastern Orthodox Ethics") to Worship (Chapter 8, "Icon and Ethics") to the Church's theology regarding Philanthropy (Chapter 9, "A Case Study in Eastern Orthodox Ethics on Rich and Poor: Alexios Makrembolites' Dialogue Between the Rich and the Poor). The 10th Chapter, "Responding to Contemporary Challenges to Orthodoxy" lifts up a number of issues of ethical and corporate identity that the Orthodox Church faces world-wide as we face the new Millennium. The final chapter of Part Two, Chapter 11, "Eastern Orthodox Ethics and Community Ethics" raises issues concerning the relationship of the Orthodox Church as community of faith and the non-ecclesial environment in which we live.

Throughout, the wholistic perspective seeks to address these topics in an integrated fashion. Because of this, these chapters do not provide ready-made recipes for living, but intend to provoke theological and ethical reflection on a broad range of Orthodox Christian existence. From Faith to Worship to Philanthropy, to Ecclesial Challenges, to the Church in a Post-Christian culture, the reader is invited to engage the full implications of the Orthodox Faith in a dialogue that may prove to be fruitful.

+S.S.H

7

THE DOCTRINE OF THE TRINITY
IN EASTERN ORTHODOX ETHICS*

The Eastern Christian understanding of the condition of humanity and salvation teaches that God, who is a Trinitarian community of divine persons who are one God, i.e., one in essence – has created the world and humanity in it. According to this teaching, humanity was created in a special and unique relationship with the Holy Trinity – in the "image and likeness of God," which the early Church in an Irenaean anthropology, understood as both a description of what it means to be a human being and the potentiality toward the realization of the "divine-like existence" in human life. This divine likeness is the goal or τέλος toward which all human beings are called to move for the fulfillment of their lives as human beings in communion with God.

This paper begins with the understanding that the Eastern Orthodox doctrine of the Trinity and the normative dimensions of the Christian life, i.e., ethics, are not only intimately related, but that the latter is rooted at its most foundational level in the former.

Further, in this paper we seek to explore the specific ways that the doctrine of the Holy Trinity illumines the ethical tradition of the Orthodox Church. As an effort at the articulation of a mystery – in the "apophatic" mode of thought – the doctrine Holy Trinity points to the complex and often paradoxical character of the ethical quest. The doctrinal tradition focusing on the structured order of the relationships of the persons of the Holy Trinity as illustrated in the *filioque* controversy in the "kataphatic" mode of thought, illumines normative patterned dimensions of inter-personal relationships. More evangelically, the Holy Trinity in Eastern Orthodox thought defines the ethical aspects of unitive love, described in patristic literature as Θεῖος ἔρως. Finally, the Holy Trinity is also a model for human God-like life in diaconal-service love, i.e., ἀγάπη, and more broadly in reference to living the God-like and God-pleasing way of life.

Doctrine and Ethics

The *Catechetical Lectures* of St. Cyril of Jerusalem (c. 347) provide an insight to the place of ethics in the faith pattern of the Church. Cyril instructed his catechumens about the relationship of belief and behavior.

> For the method of godliness consists of these two things, pious doctrines, and virtuous practice: and neither are the doctrines acceptable to God apart from good works, nor does God accept the works, which are not perfected with pious doctrines. For what profit is it, to know well the doctrines concerning God, and yet to be a vile fornicator? And again, what profit is it, to be nobly temperate, and an impious blasphemer? A most precious possession therefore is the knowledge of doctrines: also there is need of a wakeful soul, since there are many "that make spoil through philosophy and vain deceit."[1]

The "knowledge of doctrines" most certainly includes the foundations of faith that impinge upon "virtuous practice." Because, as Cyril says, "Vice mimics virtue," there is need, in addition to divine grace, "of a sober mind and eyes that see" so as to counteract the "many 'that spoil through philosophy and vain deceit.'"[2]

The point is that the ethical theory of Eastern Christianity and its doctrine affirmations form a single fabric. They are not two separate realities, though of course they may be distinguished from each other for study and exposition. Ethical behavior is inextricably bound up with belief, piety, worship, and the sacramental life. It is also inextricably bound up with growth toward God-likeness.

This Orthodox Christian approach to ethics as a discipline does for the believer and the Church regarding the moral life, what the exposition of the doctrines does for belief and worship. Both doctrine and ethics direct discernment, protect from error, and guide the Church and the individual Christian in the life of God-likeness.

Trinity, Apophaticism, Kataphaticism and Ethics

The starting point of theory in Orthodox Christian ethics is the central question of all ethical reflection, i.e., the nature of the Good. Orthodox Christian ethical theory identifies the source of all that can be identified as good with God. But the Triune God transcends in His being all human concepts. Therefore it is correct to say that God is "not good," but "above goodness" (ὑπεράγαθος). This is essentially an expression of Eastern Christian apophaticism, or negative theology. To say that God is ὑπεράγαθος in reality is a way of saying apophatically that the human mind is not able to comprehend the dimensions of God's goodness.

However, outside of this deeply apophatic approach, which is mystical and transcends all human thought, concrete things can still be said. The Old and New Testaments, and the teaching the Greek Fathers, witness to this positive understanding of the faith and its ethical application.

Theological language calls this positive way the "kataphatic approach." When speaking of God καταφατικῶς we use language from our own experience and knowledge. Gregory of Nazianzos, in his *Fifth Theological Oration* explains the use of kataphatic theological language with a measure of ingenuity.

According to Scripture, God sleeps and is awake, is angry,

walks, has the cherubim for his throne. And yet when did he become liable to passion, and have you ever heard that God has a body? This, then, is, though not really fact, a figure of speech. For we have given names according to our own comprehension from our own attributes to those of God. His remaining silent apart from us, and as it were not caring for us, for reasons known to himself, is what we call his sleeping; for our own sleep is such a state of inactivity. And again, his sudden turning to do us good is the waking up; for waking is the dissolution of sleep, as visitation is of turning away. And when he punishes, we say he is angry; for so it is with us – punishment is the result of anger. And his working, now here now there, we call walking; for walking is change from one place to another. His resting among the holy hosts, and as it were loving to dwell among them, is his sitting and being enthroned this, too, from ourselves, for God rests nowhere as he does upon the saints. His swiftness of moving is called flying, and his watchful care is called his face, and his giving and bestowing is his hand; and, in a word, every other of the powers or activities of God has depicted for us some other corporeal one.[3]

Among the aspects of divine life understood kataphatically is "goodness." As Gregory of Nyssa says, "...goodness, righteousness, wisdom and power are equally ascribed to the deity."[4] The tradition understands the Triune God as "The Good." God is thus repeatedly described in the patristic literature as the "good itself" (αὐτάγαθος). Nyssa, in his Life of Moses, teaches that "the most beautiful and supreme good of all is the Divinity itself ... whose very nature is goodness." In his Καταχητικός Λόγος Gregory speaks of God as "the highest good."[5]

Origen put it thusly: "...only in the Divine Trinity, which created all things, does goodness exist essentially (ἐνυπάρχει οὐσιωδῶς ἡ ἀγαθότης).[6]

The "Good" is the primary category of ethics. If the good cannot be known or understood in any way, then even the most simple effort to determine the quality of behavior and to articulate norms or to provide "moral oughts" for living is doomed to failure. It is an exercise in mere relativism or self-serving propaganda. Ethics as a philosophical, religious or cultural discipline that seeks to order volitional human behavior according to either what is "right," or what is "fitting and appropriate," must eventually root that ordering in some understanding and perception of what is "the good."

Numerous philosophical systems exist that seek to explicate the nature of "the good."[7] Yet, for Eastern Orthodoxy, efforts that seek to exclusively identify the good with endocosmic entities, ideas, or experiences are fundamentally false. From an Orthodox Christian perspective, the one source of goodness is the Triune God. As we shall see below, Orthodox doctrine holds to a cosmic theology that affirms the communion of the created world with God's goodness, but the created world is precisely good only in the measure of its participation in God's goodness.

The Trinity as the "Living Good"

That God is a Trinity is central to the "*theoria*" of ethics because the good is thus understood not as an abstract principle or logical construct, but as a community of persons in an ordered relationship, existing in loving communion. While it is possible to think about the good in abstract terms, as we are doing in this paper, the good itself is not abstract. The good is a living good, a reality that exists in its own right and that shares that goodness with that which outside itself, the creation. Forced to use this abstract language, theology runs the danger of "objectifying" the good and mistaking it for a concept or abstract principle. The good, however, being alive since it is identical with the living God, will not be captured, nor can it be manipulated and reduced into one-dimensional concepts or principles.

In the philosophical ethical traditions, there is a continuous effort at this form of reductionism. Whether the effort is to understand the good as natural law, as categorical imperative, as pleasure, as happiness, as utilitarian consequentialism, as some form of worldly perfectionism, or in economic terms or in evolutionary terms, or as subjective value theory or in existentialist terms, the systems prove to be inadequate. And this is so because of three reasons. These efforts are rationalist, concept-driven systems, while the good is a living, divine person, and further, a community of divine persons. These efforts are rooted in a fallen, distorted and in many ways corrupt reality, the fallen created world, while the good resides in the uncreated and incorrupt reality of God. These philosophical efforts by design more often than not consciously separate themselves from communion with the source of goodness, and therefore cannot help but be partial approaches to the good.

Yet, even for Orthodox Christian ethics the fundamental assumption the God is the good means that simple, one-dimensional, black/white moral judgments are not possible. The tendency for human beings in their quest to determine norms for their behaviors and to have clarity about "right and wrong," "fitting and unfitting," or "good and evil," may lead them to simplistic approaches to ethical issues and questions. If the good is God who is a Trinity, and that Divine Trinity is a mystery that transcends our comprehension, then the good in our experience must not be expected to be any less composed of irreducible paradoxes and antinomies. In conceptual terms ethics will seek to capture these in its decision-making. Thus, when decisions are to be made, all factors will be taken into consideration. Decision-making will consult rules and laws; it will assess good and evil consequences; it will assess intents and motives; it will judge what are appropriate means; it will ask what a decision means about values and disvalues and the development of character; and it will do so in a corporate process. But the good will not ultimately be captured with facility or in rational statements. The good for us primarily will be a reality not a concept – complex, interpenetrating, and alive.

Trinity: Structure, Pattern and Order for Ethics
Because human beings are created in the image and likeness

of God, the goodness of God is not alien or unrelated to the human condition. The good is not some sort of externally imposed law or rule. Rather, goodness in human life is iconic (reflective) of the divine goodness. By its very nature as the goodness of God who is a Trinity of persons, the good is never only privately or individualistically encountered and realized; it always has its corporate dimensions. Since growth toward God-likeness is the purpose of all creation, and especially the crown of creation – humanity – all good in the created sphere gets its content, inspiration, direction, and force from God. As a consequence, there is no independent or autonomous good. There is no good that is in substance, "secular." The good of human beings is to achieve God-likeness and in the process, to realize the human potential in its fullness.

As noted above, the good of the Holy Trinity is a living reality. When human beings are in living communion with God, they realize human good. There are several dimensions of the life of the Holy Trinity as revealed that have special application to ethics. In the first case, the relationships of the Holy Trinity are revealed having a certain structure and order. The Father is the source and "chief principle" (the Ἀρχή) of the Trinity. The Son is eternally born of the Father, and the Holy Spirit proceeds from the Father. The heresies that the early Church struggled against can be thought of as unbalancing this order and pattern. Gregory the Theologian speaks, for example, of misunderstandings of the doctrine of the Holy Trinity as Ditheism or Tritheism. In this context, note what we might call the *Trinitarian structuralism* of this passage:

> What is our quarrel and dispute with both? To us there is one God, for the Godhead is one, and all that proceeds from him is referred to one, though we believe in three Persons. For one is not more and another less God; nor is one before and another after; nor are they divided in will or parted in power; nor can you find here any of the qualities of divisible things; but the Godhead is, to speak concisely, undivided in separate Persons; and there is one min-

gling of lights, as it were of three suns joined to each other. When, then, we look at the Godhead, or the first cause, or the *monarchia*, that which we conceive is one; but when we look at the Persons in whom the Godhead dwells, and at those who timelessly and with equal glory have their being from the first cause, there are three whom we worship.[8]

In this same patterned and structured approach to the relations of the persons of the Holy Trinity, Eastern Christianity rejected the Western *filioque* ("and the Son") doctrine regarding the Holy Spirit. This doctrine teaches that the Holy Spirit proceeds from the Father and the Son. Eastern Orthodox theology holds that the *filioque* distorts the relationship of the persons of the Holy Trinity. It tends to de-personalize the Holy Spirit particularly, and the Holy Trinity as a whole.[9] The *filioque* supports a view of the Holy Spirit, not as a person in full right, but as the relationship of love between the Father and the Son, an Augustinian teaching which has seen renewed support recently.[10] This, too, has its structural, patterned and ordered dimensions.

From the Eastern view, the significance of this controversy for ethics is that there are inherent and patterned relationships appropriate to the persons of the Trinity. This means that human beings are created in the image and likeness of a God who is a Trinity of persons in concrete and specifically defined relationships. Consequently, an ethic based on becoming "God-like" must be firmly grounded in patterned relationships that indicate the appropriate behavior of human beings relative to God, neighbor, self and the rest of creation. This connection between the divine patterned order and the human need for order, pattern and structure was noted by several Fathers of the Church.

Lars Thunberg has noted such patterns in the relationship of the Holy Trinity and human nature in the teaching of St. Maximos the Confessor. In his book *Man and the Cosmos: The Vision of St. Maximus the Confessor*, Thunberg discusses the relationship of the Trinity and the constitution of man. He observes that Maximos sees parallels between the order and structure of the Trinitarian existence, and the human condition. "Thus," he observes, "the anthropological triad of 'Being,' 'Well-Being,' and 'Ever-being' is another 'adumbration' of God's Trinitarian life, and it stands in direct relation to the distinction in man between divine image and divine likeness. Consequently, one could expect to find in the very constitution of man – as an image of God, destined for likeness to Him – another 'adumbration.' In fact, we do find it even though Maximus does not develop it in detail."[11] There follows a parallel between the mind, reason and spirit of man with the three persons of the Holy Trinity. Ethically, Thunberg notes, "that the goodness expressed in the imitation of the true virtues reflects divine goodness."[12] He concludes,

> There are, therefore, in Maximus clear indications of a human *imago Trinitatis* (the image of God in man understood as an image of the Trinity), and this is related to the constitution of man and also to his spiritual potentiality ... These are only imprecise indications in an inscrutable mystery. These indications might serve as a kind of preparation for the true revelation... But, and this is important, they might also serve as a model for inner-human and inter-human relations.[13]

Thunberg correctly notes that there is a danger in pushing such parallels too far, for God is uncreated reality while humanity is creature. Yet, he observes that "at the same time it (the Trinitarian dimension) is fundamental, and it can be applied generally to all aspects of life: to creation, to the constitution of man, and to soteriology in all its phases and perspectives."[14]

Interestingly Maximos, in writing to George, the Eparch of Africa significantly exaggerating, says "...he who establishes in himself expressions of the divine characteristics, has the fullness of those things that are good, through which it is possible for persons to come to an exact likeness of God."[15]

The relationships of the Father, the Son, and the Holy Spirit are not chaotic or inchoate. There is an important, one might say, structural pattern to the relations of the Holy Trinity. This, too, is important. As Gregory of Nyssa said, "it was needful that the distinctive properties of the Father and the Son should remain peculiar to them, lest there should be confusion in the Godhead which brings all things, even disorder itself, into due arrangement and good order."[16] The patterned relationships of the Trinity, thus, may be seen as models of a certain patterned set of relationships not only within the individual human being, but also, in human social structures. To use Thunberg's significant phrase, the Trinity, also serves "as a model for inner-human and inter-human relations."

Since we are creatures, our basic structural relations will be different from those of the uncreated Trinity. But just as there are patterned relationships that may not be violated in our thoughts about the Trinity, "lest there should be confusion in the Godhead which brings all things, even disorder itself, into due arrangement and good order," so also, there are patterned moral relationships in "inter-human relationships" which cannot be violated if disorder and confusion is to be avoided.

Is there any description of these fundamental patterned moral relationships in the patristic tradition? Yes. The generic name for them is the natural moral law. The Greek Fathers understood that law in concrete terms as a low level, pan-human set of moral requirements which every person and every society has to acknowledge in order to avoid "disorder itself," and to maintain "due arrangement and good order" in human relationships. For the Eastern Church Fathers, this patterned norm for human relationships was best expressed in the Decalogue, though other expressions of it are to be found empirically in every culture and society. This is the substance of the meaning of the term "natural moral law" for the Greek Fathers.[17] Its connection with Trinitarian theology is not so much in its content. The association of the two is rather in the parallel between the ordered structure of the relationship of the persons of the Godhead, on the one hand, and the pattern of the natural moral law in human social relations, on the other.

Trinity: Communion of Persons – Θεῖος Ἔρως

Significant for ethics, as well, is the relationship of the persons of the Holy Trinity, which we seek to understand in the concept of the mutual love of the three divine persons. Here too, we deal with a mystery which we seek to express in comprehensible terms. "Love" is best apprehended by the human soul only in the experience of loving God and knowing His love for us.

To say "God is love" is to make, at once, a statement about the Holy Trinity in Itself, and about God's *energies* (grace) toward His creatures. According to the Scriptures, the three persons of the Holy Trinity relate to and among each other in love. Because of this, God is love. Additionally, because God relates to us – His creatures – in a loving way, God is love. Because we are created in the image of a loving God, and we are called to achieve the fullness of life by becoming increasingly God-like, the ethical requirement exists for us to love. Thus, there is a love-ethic for human beings, based on the goal of God-likeness. Humans have a moral imperative to love God, the neighbor, ourselves, and the creation, in appropriate and fitting ways. In this basic framework is to be found the rest of the Christian ethic. This love then, may be differentiated in two forms. The first is unitive-love, or as it has come to be known, *eros*-love. The other is diaconal love, known as *agape*-love. In this section we address the concept of *eros* or unitive love, as it is expressed in Orthodox Trinitarian theology.

In recent years, Orthodox thought about the Holy Trinity has focused on the inner agapaic relations of the three persons. This emphasis has come to the fore in the writings of Vladimir Lossky, Bishop John Zizioulas, Christos Yannaras, and many others.[18]

This movement has been strongly influenced on the one hand by Byzantine ascetic and monastic traditions and on the other by contemporary existentialist thought. This contemporary Orthodox emphasis has sought to formulate the classical theological understandings of the divine οὐσία (essence) and the divine ὑποστάσεις (hypostases) or πρόσωπα (persons) in a way that divests the term οὐσία from essentialist connotations, identifying the θεῖα οὐσία (divine essence) with the agapaic relationships of the three persons of the Trinity. According to Zizioulas, the terms "person" and "hypostasis" came to mean the same thing in Orthodox mainline theology in the Christological struggles of the fourth century. In this view, personhood is not understood as a consequence of being, but the person is the very hypostasis of being. The constitutive element of divine being is personhood.

Consequently, οὐσία is not to be understood as existing separately from πρόσωπον. By definition, the divine essence is the divine existence in personhood. The source of the Trinity, thus, is the person of the Father, not a commonly shared in objective divine essence–*ousia*. Fatherhood in the Trinity implies relationship with the Son and the Holy Spirit, which goes beyond structured patterns of relationship. This perspective in its most strongly stated form does not understand the pattern of the Father as "source" of the other two persons of the Trinity, the Son as "forever born" of the Father and the Holy Spirit as "forever proceeding" from the Father in ordered and patterned categories. Rather, these relationships are the result of the freedom of the Father, in this manner overcoming a supposed ontological necessity in the divine οὐσία. The second and third persons of the Holy Trinity come into being through the free choice of the Father as a person because the Father desires this communion.

The nature of this communion is one of unitive love, a perichoretic relationship of mutual inter-penetration and unbroken union. Thus, in only one way does the Father differ from the Son, in that the second person of the Trinity is born of the Father. Similarly, in only one way does the Father differ from the Spirit, in that the third person of the Trinity proceeds from the Father. In all other ways, willing, choosing, acting, the persons function communionally and unitively. This inter-relation of the persons of the Trinity are characterized as a "divine eros," θεῖος ἔρως, which constitutes the completion and fulfillment of a personal Trinitarian communion.[19]

The ethical implications of this emphasis are enormous. If this understanding is correct as an exclusive understanding of the Holy Trinity, then it implies that anything appearing to be a heteronomous norm, a structured requirement for existence is false and an unauthentic imposition upon free spirits created in the image and likeness of God. Rules, commands, social networks, natural moral law, and the like have no place. Freedom of choice in communion with the living God as θεῖος ἔρως is the heart of ethical living. Hence, Yannaras' book title, The *Freedom of Morality.*

This perspective on the Trinity has come under criticism as of late. A monastic theologian, Gabriel Dionysiates, has rejected this version of Trinitarian theology as the basis of Orthodox monastic practice. A biblical theologian, Savas Agourides, has critiqued it for its lack of historicity and its disregard for the Christian salvation *heilesgeschichte.* This author, as an ethicist, has questioned the historicity and the theological integrity of some of the ethical conclusions of this approach, as well as its dependence on philosophical existentialism as incompatible with the whole pattern of biblical and patristic ethical styles.[20] It is not the place here to enter into this debate.

Nevertheless, it would be hard to gainsay that this approach has served to lift up the meaning of unitive love (ἔρως) as not only present in the Trinity, but also as a τέλος for human moral behavior. The Scriptural basis is too rich, the theology of communion with God in the Church, and Christian concern for peace, harmony, and pan-human union is too well documented to question the emphasis on love as communion as an authentic component of Orthodox Ethics. This is in contrast to Anders Nygren's Protestant rejection of *eros*–love.[21] Trinitarian considerations (not, of course, uninfluenced by Platonism and Neoplatonism), lead not only Orthodox ethics, but the whole of the Orthodox worldview and ethos, to an affirmation of unitive-love as essential. At its root is the Johannine approach to the relationship of the Father, the Son and the Holy Spirit.

Thus, in John 10.30 the fundamental Trinitarian affirmation is revealed: "I and the Father are one." Further, Jesus declares "that I love the Father."[22] The perichoretic character of love, understood as θεῖος ἔρως, i.e. communion and mutual fellowship, is reflected in 1 John 1.3: "...that which we have seen and heard we proclaim also to you, so that you may have fellowship with us; and our fellowship is with the Father and with his Son Jesus Christ." Similarly, in the next chapter mutual love of Christians is related with faith in both the Son and the work of the Spirit. We read:

> (If) we love one another, God abides in us and his love is perfected in us.
> By this we know that we abide in him and he in us, because he has given us of his own Spirit.
> And we have seen and testify that the Father has sent his Son as the Savior of the world.
> Whoever confesses that Jesus is the Son of God, God abides in him, and he in God.
> So we know and believe the love God has for us. God is love, and he who abides in love abides in God, and God abides in him.[23]

Similarly, we are alerted to the perichoretic mutual abiding character of love, differentiated in the Tradition by the term ἔρως in 1 John 2.24: "Let what you heard from the beginning abide in you. If what you heard from the beginning abides in you, then you will abide in the Son and in the Father." No clearer articulation of it is to be found than that in the Great High Priestly Prayer of Jesus recorded in the 17th chapter of the Fourth Gospel (vv. 21-23). Jesus prays

> ... that they may all be one; even as thou, Father, art in me, and I in thee, that they also may be in us, so that the world may believe that thou hast sent me. The glory which thou hast given me I have given to them, that they may be one even as we are one, I in them and thou in me, that they may become perfectly one, so that the world may know that thou hast sent me and hast loved them even as thou hast loved me.

This unitive love is intimately connected with ethical behavior. The strong implication in the Johannine corpus is that one cannot claim communion with the Trinitarian God if morally categorized behavior is not in harmony with the divine life and will of the Trinity. Thus, Jesus says of himself, "I do as the Father has commanded me, so that the world may know that I love the Father."[24]

Thus, interestingly and by way of digression, in these Johannine passages one finds some of the strongest arguments against an exclusively existential understanding of love and Christian ethics broadly conceived. Following commandments, for existentialist ethics, is by definition "unauthentic." At this point, we can only wonder what this does to a Trinitarian theology, which sees only freedom in the relationships of the persons of the Trinity.

I would hold that the Johannine approach to unitive love corrects an exclusive dependence upon it for Orthodox Christian ethics. Thus, "He who says 'I know him' but disobeys his commandments is a liar, and the truth is not in him; but whoever keeps his word, in him truly love for God is perfected. By this we may be sure that we are in him: he who says he abides in him ought to walk in the same way in which he walked."[25] The obverse would seem to be also true. The commandments can only be fulfilled when the human being is in communion with God.

I conclude this section with a final Johannine passage that shows the interplay of unitive factors in the Trinity, their modeling for human beings created in the image and likeness of the God who is a Trinity, and the decisive relationship of works of love in maintaining the communion. The passage comes from the Fourth Gospel's 14th chapter in response to Philip's request of Jesus that he show the Father to the Disciples.

"Do you not believe that I am in the Father and the Father in me? The words that I say to you I do not speak on my own authority; but the Father who dwells in me does his works. Believe me that I am in the Father and the Father in me; or else believe me for the sake of the works themselves.

Truly, truly, I say to you, he who believes in me will also do the works that I do; and greater works than these will he do, because I go to the Father. Whatever you ask in my name, I will do it, that the Father may be glorified in the Son; if you ask anything in my name, will do it.

If you love me, you will keep my commandments. And I will pray the Father, and he will give you another Counselor, to be with you for ever, even the Spirit of truth…"[26]

Trinity, Diaconal-Agape Love and Ethics

The relationship of diaconal love, ἀγάπη in the strict sense of the term as used here, does not need extensive documentation. Scripture and Patristic tradition are clear, and little controversy accompanies the idea that the love of God the Father for His creatures and the love of Jesus Christ for humanity and communion with the Holy Spirit create models for human behavior.

Ἀγάπη as diaconal love is service to meet the needs of another without motives which look toward recompense. In my own work I describe this form of divine love for humankind as characterized by "self-less benevolence."[27] This form of love is not focused on the inner unitive eros-love of the persons of the Trinity, but on the divine energies of the Holy Trinity as they flow outward to create, sustain, redeem, and sanctify the creation, and humanity in particular.

Again, a short excursus to the Johannine tradition is instructive. I share with you a passage from another writing of mine on the subject of diaconal agape-love.

> If we are to understand the meaning of agape we will do well by starting from a passage in the 1st Epistle of John: "herein is love, not that we loved God, but that He loved us." This passage is the key. If we really want to know what love is about, we are going to have to turn our attention to God. We are going to have to ask how God has dealt with us. How has agape-love as it exists in God been

expressed toward us? 1 John informs us: "Herein was the love of God manifested in us, that God has sent his only-begotten Son into the world that we might live through him." The greatest act of love was to give to (hu)mankind the means to become once again what (hu)mankind was originally designed to be... "For God so loved the world that he gave his only-begotten Son, that whoever believes in Him should not perish but have eternal life. For God sent the Son into the world, not to condemn the world, but that the world might be saved through Him."[28]

These Trinitarian actions create moral obligations on the part of those who receive them. In the biblical and patristic tradition, Christians are not only recipients of these actions. The Trinitarian outpouring of love is to be responded to not only with gratitude and acceptance.

Trinitarian love provokes normative requirements for similar behavior on the part of Christians. The ethical "ought" language for human behavior is rooted in Trinitarian outreaching *agape*-love. Again, the Johannine literature may serve to illustrate. In 1 John 3.16 the pronouncement is made that "By this we know love, that he laid down his life for us; and we ought to lay down our lives for the brethren." In 1 John 4.7-11, the redemptive work of God's love for humanity expresses itself in the moral requirement that human beings ought to love one another.

> Beloved, let us love one another; for love is of God, and he who loves is born of God and knows God. He who does not love does not know God; for God is love. In this the love of God was made manifest among us, that God sent his only Son into the world, so that we might live through him. In this is love, not that we loved God but that he loved us and sent his Son to be the expiation for our sins. Beloved, if God so loved us, we also ought to love one another.

It is not only 1 Corinthians 13 that indicates that other virtues are rooted in Christian love. Perhaps Maximos the Confessor can represent the patristic vision on this point. In his second letter[29] that has the theme of love, he asks "which form of all that is good is not contained (κέκτηται) by love?" He proceeds to incorporate into love, faith, hope, humility ("the first basis of the virtues"), gentleness, forbearance, self-control, patience, long-suffering, goodness, peace, and joy into love.[30] He concludes that love "is their fulfillment embracing entirely the supreme desirable in its totality and providing for them the rest of their movement towards it…"[31] In this motif is also to be noted the tradition of the imitation of God and Christ. Orthodox ethicist George Mantzarides has made a special study of the tradition of the imitation of God and Christ in the Orthodox tradition. The "God-likeness" tradition of *theosis* is, of course, its theological foundation.[32]

In the New Testament the concept is restricted to the Pauline corpus. While Jesus calls His disciples to "follow him," Paul calls upon Christians to imitate God and Christ, with occasional reference to the activity of the Holy Spirit. There is one passage in 1 Peter that speaks of Jesus' example of suffering which is to be followed by Christians: "…if when you do right and suffer for it (and) you take it patiently, you have God's approval. For to this you have been called, because Christ also suffered for you, leaving you an example that you should follow in his steps."[33]

The clearest Pauline exhortation to imitate God the Father and Christ is in Ephesians: "Therefore be imitators of God, as beloved children. And walk in love, as Christ loved us and gave himself up for us, a fragrant offering and sacrifice to God."[34] Several times Paul exhorts his followers to imitate him as an imitator of Christ. Thus, to the Corinthians he writes "I urge you, then, be imitators of me"[35] and "Be imitators of me, as I am of Christ."[36] In several places he recommends his behavior for imitation and commends his readers for following it, noting that their imitation of his imitation of Christ has become an example for others to imitate![37]

Mantzarides shows that this motif of imitation of God, of

Christ, and of the saints continued in the Eastern Christian tradition. He writes:[38]

> According to Clement of Alexandria, Christianity teaches one "to live in the imitating power of God (πολιτεύεσθαι εἰς δύναμιν ἐξομοιωτικήν τῷ Θεῷ)."[39] St. Gregory of Nyssa defines Christianity as "the imitation of the divine nature."[40] St. Basil says that the "rule" (ὅρος) of Christianity is the imitation of Christ "in the measure of the incarnation."[41] Finally, St. Maximos the Confessor considers the imitation of Christ as an self-evident expression of the love of the believer for Him. "A person who loves Christ," he says, "unquestionably imitates Him as much as he is able."[42]

Conclusion

This paper has sought to show that the ethical, normative tradition in Eastern Orthodox Christianity is rooted in the Holy Trinity. We have sought to show that this is not come by through a process of rigid rational deduction, but as an outgrowth of the living goodness of the Holy Trinity and the creation of humanity in the "image and likeness of God." This theological affirmation is at the heart of Orthodox Christian Ethics. Assuming a divine like freedom, or to use the more accurate patristic word *autexousion* (αὐτεξούσιον), i.e. "self-determination," ethics has as its anthropological base the given of the divine image in human beings, and the potentiality of growth toward God-likeness, or *theosis*. The first theologian of the Church, Origen, put it this way:

> The highest good, to which every rational nature hastens, is also called the "end of all that is." ...(T)he highest good is to become, as far as possible, similar to God .... Moses asserts: "Let us make man in our own image and likeness." Then he adds, "and God did make man, and in the image of God he made him."

> The fact that in this last sentence the prophet speaks of God making man in his "image," but is silent about his

"likeness" means nothing less than that man received the dignity of the divine image in his original condition. The perfection of God's likeness was delayed for the end so that man himself might achieve it through the efforts of his striving to imitate God. He then had a possibility of perfecting himself that was granted in the beginning through the dignity of the divine image. In the end, through the exertion of his efforts, he might achieve for himself a perfect likeness of God.[43]

Origen continues, and in some measure also defines what eventually came to be called the discipline of Christian Ethics, when he added, "Hence, we must inquire diligently what is this perfection of beatitude and the end of all things, when we say that, not only is God in all things, but is all in all things."[44]

We have explored the unitive love of the Holy Trinity as a model for the ethical relationships of human beings with God and with one another. We have examined in brief the diaconal agapaic model of the persons of the Holy Trinity as the model for the *agape*-love among Christians. It was not possible in this brief context to spell all of the aspects of this kind of love in Christian ethics, but the paper sought to lift up the inclusion of the virtues in the life of love found in the Holy Trinity. As a conclusion, the imitation of God, Christ was lifted up as another expression of the Trinitarian basis for Eastern Orthodox ethics.

Through this exercise, it is hoped that the ethical dimension of the spiritual life of the Christian's communion with the Trinitarian God has been demonstrated.

All who keep (God's) commandments abide in him, and he in them. And by this we know that he abides in us, by the Spirit which he has *given us*.[45]

ENDNOTES

* Presented at the Annual Meeting of the American Academy of Religion in 1990, at New Orleans, LA. It was part of the session of the

Eastern Orthodox Studies Consultation on the theme "The Doctrine of the Trinity in Eastern Orthodox Thought."

[1]Cyril of Jerusalem, *Catechetical Lectures*, IV, 2, *Nicene and Post-Nicene Fathers. Second Series*, Vol. VII, p. 19. The biblical verse quoted is Colossians 2.8.

[2]Ibid., IV, 1.

[3]St. Gregory of Nazianzos, *Fifth Theological Oration*, sec. 22, in *Christology of the Later Fathers*, ed. E. R. Hardy and C. Richardson. Vol. III of the *Library of Christian Classics*. Philadelphia: The Westminster Press, 1953, p. 207.

[4]*Address on Religious Instruction (Κατηχητικὸς Λόγος)*, Introduction, *Christology of Later Fathers*, ibid., p. 270.

[5] *Περὶ τοῦ Βίου Μωυσέως*, MPG, 44, 301. *Address on Religious Instruction*, op. cit., sec. 15, p. 203.

[6] *Περὶ Ἀρχῶν*, I, 6. 2.

[7]See Stanley S. Harakas, *Toward Transfigured Life: The* Theoria *of Eastern Orthodox Ethics*. Minneapolis: Light and Life Publishing Co., 1983, ch. 3.

[8]*Fifth Theological Oration*, op. cit., sec. 14, p. 202.

[9]For a good, yet non-technical exposition of this Eastern view, see Timothy Ware, The *Orthodox Church*, Baltimore: Penguin Books, 1966, Ch. 11. For a more theological and technical treatment, see Vladimir Lossky, *Mystical Theology*, op. cit., ch. 3. For a discussion of the point from Eastern and Roman Catholic perspectives, see, *Trinitarian Theology: East and West*, by Michael A. Fahey and John Meyendorff, Brookline, MA., Holy Cross Orthodox Press, 1977.

[10]See David Coffey, "The Holy Spirit as the Mutual Love of the Father and the Son," *Theological Studies*, June, 1990, vol. 51, no. 2, pp. 193-229.

[11]Crestwood, NY: St. Vladimir's Seminary Press, 1985, p. 47.

[12]Ibid.

[13]Ibid., pp. 47-48.

[14]Ibid., p. 48.

[15] *Λόγος παραινετικὸς ἐν εἴδῃ ἐπιστολῆς πρὸς τὸν δοῦλον τοῦ Θεοῦ Γεώργιον*. MPG, 91, 365. The text of this passage reads as follows: "Ὁ γὰρ τῶν θείων ἰδιωμάτων ἑαυτοῦ κατὰ τὸν βίον τὰς ἐμφάσεις καταστήσας γνωρίσματα, πάντων ἐντελῶς ἔχει τόν ἀγαθῶν πλήρωμα δι' οὗ πέφυκεν ἐγγίνεσθαι τοῖς

ἀνθρώποις ἡ πρὸς τὸν Θεὸν ἀκριβὴς ἐξομοίωσις."

[16]Gregory Nazianzos, *Fifth Theological Oration*, op. cit., sec 29 p. 211.

[17]See Harakas, *Toward Transfigured Life*, op. cit., ch. 6 for a full treatment of the concept of the natural moral law in the Greek Fathers.

[18]Vladimir Lossky, *The Mystical Theology of the Eastern Church*. London: James Clarke and Co., 1957. John Zizioulas, *Being as Communion*. London: 1985. Christos Yannaras, *The Freedom of Morality*. Crestwood, NY: St. Vladimir's Seminary Press, 1977.

[19]While this summary is mine, I have been helped in formulating it by a similar summary by Professor Savas Agourides' article "Can the Persons of the Trinity Provide Bases for Personalistic Views of Man?" (Greek) in Σύναξης, Jan-Mar, 1990, pp. 67-78.

[20]Gabriel Dionysiates, ῾Η Αἵρεσις τῶν ΝεοΟρθοδόξων· ῾Ο Νεονικολαϊτισμὸς τοῦ Χρη. Γιανναρά. Orthodoxos Typos Publications, 1988; Savas Agourides, Ibid. Stanley S. Harakas, op. cit., pp. 59-65.

[21]*Agape and Eros*, New York: Harper and Row, 1969.

[22]John 14.31.

[23]1 John 4.12-16.

[24]John 14.31.

[25]1 John 2.4-6.

[26]John 14.10-16.

[27]Harakas, op. cit., ch. 7.

[28]Ibid., p. 60. John 4.10, 1 John 4.9, John 3.16-17.

[29]Πρὸς Ἰωάννην κουβικουλάριον, περὶ ἀγάπης, MPG 91, 392-408.

[30]Ibid., pp. 393-396.

[31]Translation by Lars Thunberg, op.cit., p. 105.

[32]George Mantzarides, Χριστιανικὴ Ἠθικὴ (Christian Ethics). 2nd Edition. Thessalonike: P. Pournaras Publications, n.d., ch. 14.

[33]1 Peter 2.20-21.

[34]Ephesians 5.1-2.

[35]1 Corinthians 4.16.

[36]1 Corinthians 11.1.

[37]For example, in 1 Cor. 4.17 "Therefore I send to you Timothy, my beloved and faithful child in the Lord, to remind you of my ways in Christ, as I teach them everywhere in every church;" In 1 Thessalonians

1.2 and 5-6, "And you became imitators of us and of the Lord, for you received the word in much affliction, with joy;" and "And you became imitators of us and of the Lord, for you received the word in much affliction, with joy inspired by the Holy Spirit; so that you became an example to all the believers in Macedonia and in Achaia."

[38]Op. cit., p. 159.

[39]Στρωματεῖς 1,11,52.

[40] Πρὸς Χαρμώνιον 4, MPG 45, 244D.

[41]Longer Rules 43, MPG 31,1028BC.

[42]*Chapters on Love.* 4, 55, HPG 90, 1060C.

[43]*On First Principles* 3, 6, 1.

[44]Ibid.

[45]1 John 3.24.

8

ICON AND ETHICS*

The perception that "Icon" and "Ethics" have little if anything to do with each other, I am sure reflects a broad and general perspective widespread both inside and outside the Orthodox Church today.[1] For many, the relationship between the two would appear to be non-existent, and such persons would unabashedly question the possibility that any significant connection between the two could be found at all. Others might be intrigued by the concept, yet suggest that it might be a strain on one's creativity to formulate any connection between the icon and ethics.

What I propose to do in this paper is, first, to minimize my "creativity" as much as possible by examining the sources of the Orthodox tradition in regard to icons and ethics to see if a relationship does exist between them in the tradition's theological and historical contexts. Secondly, assuming that such a tradition exists, I want to make some suggestions as to why a "forgetfulness" of that tradition has occurred both within the Orthodox tradition and outside of it, and to suggest the need for it to be reclaimed for our times. Finally, I *will* use *some* imagination in drawing out some ethical axioms from the icon, and in proposing concrete ways by which icon and ethics may serve each other in contemporary ethical teaching and church life.

ETHICS AND ICONS IN THE EASTERN CHRISTIAN TRADITION

Is there a connection between the icon as it is understood in Eastern Christian tradition and its ethical teaching? One of the presuppositions required to answer the question is the need to recognize the complexity of the development of the Orthodox theology of the icon as it faced various trends and emphases in the counter-development of the iconoclastic theological tradition.

It might be helpful to very briefly outline the history of the controversy regarding icons in the 8th century in the Byzantine Empire, and to briefly define the approach to ethics and the foundational theological tradition of Orthodoxy concerning icons at the beginning of this paper for the sake of providing a general context of the discussion which is to follow. In addition, note will have to be taken of various kinds of theological positions in the iconoclastic controversy so as to understand the history of the relationship of ethics and the icon.

The Iconoclastic Controversy[2]

For most Eastern Orthodox theologians and historians of the iconoclastic controversy, the issue regarding the use or the abolishment of icons was always much more than a difference of interpretation of the commandment regarding idols. The iconodules, the venerators of icons, saw in the icons a theological affirmation of Orthodox truth, while the iconoclasts, literally, the icon smashers, were motivated by suspicions that any art with a religious subject was suspect and dangerous. What was an affirmation of the creation and the incarnation for the first, was a return to idolatry for the second. Some see an inordinate Moslem influence on the iconoclasts, while others discern an inordinate Greek pagan influence on the iconodules. Most are agreed that the iconoclastic controversy involved much more than these influences: it at heart was a dispute not primarily about art, but about "the character of Christ's human nature, the Christian attitude towards matter, the true meaning of

Christian redemption," in the characterization of Bishop Ware.[3]

The controversy began in 726 when Emperor Leo III began his attack on the icons. It ended 120 years later when in 843 Empress Theodora restored the icons, in what has since come to be called the "Triumph of Orthodoxy," celebrated annually in Orthodox Churches on the first Sunday of Great Lent as the "Sunday of Orthodoxy." Between those two dates, two phases of the controversy were played out.

The end of the first period of controversy was what is now known as the 7th Ecumenical Council (also, as 2nd Nicaea) which in 787 proclaimed a doctrine of icons which has become normative for the Orthodox Church.

Icons serve both as teaching devices for the unlettered and as "windows on heaven," concrete embodiments of the incarnational and transfiguring truths of the Christian faith. In honoring the icon, the honor is passed on to the prototype; therefore it is in no way perceived to have anything to do with idolatry. The form of the icon is not designed to portray the concrete this-worldly fallen and distorted empirical created re-ality. Rather, it seeks to convey the fulfilled and transfigured eschatological reality of the heavenly kingdom. This explains the unusual draftsmanship, such as the inverted perspective, the prominence of the open eyes in saintly figures, the lavish use gold and other precious metals, and a stylized method of depic-tion. In the West, Eastern Christian iconography was widely misunderstood until the advent of modern art. The insights of this new approach which rejected decadent photographic art, paradoxically provoked new appreciation for the Eastern Chris-tian icon.

However, during the eighth and ninth centuries, in the process of defending the icons, Orthodox writers developed varying theological perspectives in accordance to the kind of opposition they faced from the iconoclasts. Thus, differing though neither contradictory nor mutually exclusive theologies of the icon developed. Certain of these theological streams can provide light on the issue of the relationship of the icon to ethics. Other theological perspectives developed by the iconodules were not so conducive to an ethical approach to icons.

There remains the task of briefly defining the terms, "Ethics" and "Icon" as they are understood and used in this paper.

Ethics

When we speak of Christian Ethics we speak of that aspect of the Christian Faith which articulates its normative, "ought" dimension. We are referring to those aspects of the Orthodox tradition which make claims on the will, the choosing ability human beings have, based in the "self-determining freedom" of our human nature, and in particular, the Christian believer.

Though Orthodox Christians do not often focus on the normative dimensions of their Faith, when such attention is given, almost every dimension of Orthodoxy reveals that some aspect of ethics is present. The direction and guidance, the commandments and rules, the prescriptions and the proscriptions, which are integral parts of the Christian tradition, are the specific content of its ethical tradition. In Orthodox Christianity, these normative statements are embodied in Scripture, in the patristic exegesis of Scripture, the larger patristic and conciliar tradition, the canons, the monastic *typika* and the tradition of spiritual exercise (ἄσκησις and ἀγών), the sermonic tradition, the prayer tradition, the liturgy and worship, even the architecture of the church structure.[4]

Doctrinally, this normative "ought" is rooted in the beliefs of Orthodoxy in the Trinitarian nature of God, in the creation of humanity in the image and likeness of God, in the fallen condition of humanity, in the restoration of the image and the call to its fulfillment in the "likeness," in short, the renewal in freedom of the human God-likeness, in deification. This goal of human life is approached in a multiplicity of ways: theological, sacramental, liturgical, spiritual, but also ethical.[5]

As Vladimir Lossky put it, "To be the image of God, the Fathers affirm, in the last analysis is to be a personal being, that is, to say, a free responsible being. Why, one may ask, did God create man free and responsible? Precisely because He wanted to call him to a supreme vocation: deification; that is to say, to become by grace... as God. And this call demands a free response..."[6] Elsewhere, Lossky points to the eschatological truth that the "realization of the last end, by the grace of the Holy Spirit and by human freedom, is the inner mystery of the Church... The mystery of deification which is being fulfilled in the Church is eschatology at work..."[7] One could take this apt phrase and say that for Orthodoxy, ethics (i.e., the normative dimension of the faith) is "eschatology at work," i.e., realizing the "Kingdom life" in the here and now.

Though it affirms and uses rules, commandments, proscriptions and prescriptions, Orthodox Ethics has little in common with the autonomous Kantian ethics of traditional Protestantism, nor the naturalistic "probablism" of classic Roman Catholicism; and though there is a strong affirmation of human freedom in its teaching, Orthodox Ethics has little in common with the existentialist subjectivism of much of present day Protestantism and Roman Catholicism.[8]

Icons

Numerous themes are discussed by all the theologians and historians of the iconoclastic controversy: the icon as witness and embodiment of the transfiguration of matter; the redemption of creation; and icons as witnesses to the divinized, eschatological, transfigured reality.[9] While one side of the theological discussion of the icon seeks to interpret the icon as a pointer God-ward, as a vision of the transfigured cosmos in its form and purpose, another trend in iconologic theology has looked the other way, in terms of the impact of the icon on the believer, and the message imparted to the person who gazes upon the icon. Of course, the two are connected and relate to each other intimately. But the former emphasis is the most dominant. Few Orthodox theologians today concern themselves very much with the dimension of the icon's relationship to the believer.

Among these, probably no one has articulated this more fully than has Dumitru Staniloae, the Romanian Orthodox systematic theologian, in his remarkable chapter "Revelation Through Acts, Words, and Images."[10] Responding to recent developments in biblical theology regarding the revelatory character of the Holy Scriptures, Staniloae, as he speaks of revelation through images, recognizes the contingent character of specific images, but also points to what he calls the "objective core" of the image, which is apprehended in part in a "non-subjective" way, serving to mold the whole person who observes it.

As an image, Staniloae presents the icon as having this kind of impression and influence upon the believer. In fact, precisely as icon and not mere picture, the icon is seen as serving a purpose of formation, not based on subjective emotions or imaginations, but upon the objective reality of the divine-human reality which the Christian is called to realize in life. Staniloae's comments are thus pertinent to our search for the relationship between ethics and the icon. He first makes an affirmation of the "objective" character of the image presented.

> Words must always be rooted in the perfect image of God which is the humanity of Christ, that is, Christ as man. The icons of Christ serve this same purpose... It might seem that there is contradiction between the Fathers' statement that the faithful must be careful not to force the formation of an image of Christ in their imagination, and the assertion of the value of icons. In fact, the Christian is liable to introduce subjective elements taken from his own interior imagination into the image of Christ, and these may well represent a decline from the true image of Christ. It is for this reason that icons are always painted according to fixed canons, which make no allowance for the addition of even the least subjective element.[11]

This presentation in acts, words, and images, and in particular, in the icon, of an "objective" Christ, however raises a question: to what purpose is this presentation made?

Ethics and Icons: The Question

This is precisely the nexus where ethics as we have understood it above and the icon occurs. The question is, put differently, "Is there a normative purpose to the icon?" Does the icon not only present a truth, but also present to the believer who stands before it an "ought" which addresses his or her freedom and does it seek a response? Do we speak only of aesthetic appreciation, or even only of the communication of information, or does the icon make a demand upon the believer who witnesses it for what it is, an icon and not a mere picture?

Staniloae sees the image as making such a demand, which seems to create a substantive connection between icon and ethics on the level of human *telos*, the goal toward which we ought to be moving as human beings. He continues,

> This fidelity to Christ whose humanity is the real and definitive image of God, and the formation of the faithful according to this image, are both maintained and achieved through the imitation of his acts in the sacraments, and in the entire effort at imitation of him, and it achieves to a certain extent what was intended by his own acts, the more so as the effort is aided by energy (i.e. divine grace) radiating from him whom the faithful desire to imitate, and who already exists in that risen state which the faithful yearn to share by patterning their own acts on his.[12]

In short, the image of Christ in the icon is a provocation which calls for a response on the part of the beholder to make real in himself or herself what the icon presents for contemplation and veneration. From this comes the educative dimension of the icon.

Icons as Didactic

In speaking of the "word" (not the icon), Staniloae specifically sees a normative relationship between the giver of the word and the receiver. He says:

> The human word corresponds to the divine reality not

only as meaning become conscious in man, but in a more complete manner, as discernment of the divine command and response to it. In the encounter with the divine reality the whole man experiences himself as one engaged in a dialogue with God as a partner obedient and responsible to the divine word. The whole man is thus moulded as an obedient and responsive being in the encounter with God, and the experience of these qualities causes the word to spring up in him as a remembrance in human form of the divine word, and as a response to it. This is the experience of man as one who carries the impress of God and yet is at the same time distinct from him."[13]

Were this same thought pattern carried over to the icon, it would establish the normative character of the icon as well. For "a partner with God" who is "obedient and responsible" implies an exercise of freedom and choice which is nothing other than ethical.

Nevertheless, modern Orthodox writers have not, by and large chosen to develop the theology of the icon as far as that. At most, they have affirmed what must be a preliminary dimension of the discussion regarding icon and ethics, its didactic character. This is important, because it focuses, even if in a small way, on the dimension of the icon, which points toward the worshipping viewer rather than toward the divine.

Even abbreviated and popular accounts of the icon, such as that of Bishop Ware in his *The Orthodox Church,* make mention of the didactic character of the icons for the people of God.[14] But the major focus of such treatments is nearly always on the doctrine of the distinction between λατρεία (worship) and τιμή (honor), the "movement of the honor" from the icon to the "prototype," and the impact of the doctrine of the icon on the potential sanctity of matter, its transfiguration, the redemption of creation, and the icon as a foretaste of the transfigured cosmos.[15]

So also Sahas eloquently points to the didactic nature of the icon in his book *Icon and Logos.* Thus, icons

serve to 'articulate' and accentuate the word of the Scriptures and the theology of the Church. They serve as a means
of spiritual elevation and an instrument of instruction,
not only for the illiterate, but even for the literate ones
who want, however, to penetrate beyond the realm of the
word and reason...as the word became a means of instruction through hearing, so did the icon through vision.[16]

As such, in Sahas' apt phrase, the icon was "an act of the
Church for the Church."[17] He quotes Fotis Kontoglou, the pre-
mier modern Orthodox iconographer, who says that the icons
"do not aim only at decorating a church with paintings in order
for it to be aesthetically attractive and pleasant to the worship-
pers... but rather in order to elevate them to the mystical world
of faith..."[18]

Sahas does, however indicate something of a normative tone
to the icon, if only indirectly. In comparing the icon with Re-
naissance religious painting, he describes it in these "almost ethical" terms: "The Byzantine icon is lean and fasting; it is a statement of faith and of a certain ethos that expresses what is rich in
poverty, humility, contrition, with a disposition to the quest for
sanctity."[19] However, here the "quest for sanctity" is in the icon,
not a provocation for response in the observing worshipper.

George Mantzarides, Professor of Orthodox Ethics at the
University of Thessalonike, also skirts the normative dimension
of the icon. While affirming that the human being "is a living
icon of God,"[20] so that he stands in an affinity of relationships
with the only true icon of God, the Son, and the saints and,
therefore, also with the icon, it is the saints which interest him
most, even as he speaks of icons in his Ethics text.

Mantzarides draws an analogy between the *Synaxaria* (i.e.
the lives) of the saints and the icons, both of which call for a
mimesis or imitation by the Christians. "In the lives of the saints,"
he says, "we have something analogous to byzantine iconography. And this is natural, since the saints as 'living icons' of the
life according to God, present before us the imitation of good
works."[21] The main purpose of both, according to Mantzarides,

is "to give us an idea of the new creation."[22] This is not to be denied, but his treatment does not move beyond the informational. It does not carry with it a normative ring.

Vladimir Lossky, in his chapter on the "Theology of the Image"[23] makes a case for the centrality of the theology of the image in theology. "There is no branch of theological teaching which can be entirely isolated from the problem of the image without danger of severing it from the living stock of Christianity."[24]

He clearly meant this in the broadest of understandings, but it holds true as well for our question. The concept of the image certainly is central to Orthodox Christian ethics. As he himself said, "Man created 'in the image' is the person capable of manifesting God in the extent to which his nature allows itself to be penetrated by deifying grace. Thus the image – which is inalienable – can become similar or dissimilar, to the extreme limits; that of union with God...or indeed, that of the extremity of falling away." If the icon is by definition "penetrated by divine grace" the ethical impact of it upon the other "icon of God," the free image of God who can choose to respond or reject its message, might have been drawn in this passage by Lossky, but it was not.

These examples in contemporary Orthodox theology could be multiplied many times over. What we see in much of current theological approaches in the Orthodox Church from these examples is that the ethical connection with the icon is incipiently present, but is hardly ever articulated by modern Orthodox theology.

Where is it possible to find an expression of such a connection? I believe that it is to be found in the patristic tradition, which awaits our re-discovery of it.

Icons as Normative

In this paper, the word "normative" designates not a legal, essentially heteronomous demand arising from a moral order extraneous to the ethical subject, as it often does in classical western Christian traditions. Rather, "normative" points to the *telos* and goal of human life, divine-likeness, or *theosis*. This Eastern Christian perspective sees the "norm" of human behavior in the "being" of human behavior, i.e., the image of God which is the true and full meaning of our humanity. From this perspective, the issue for us in this paper is whether the icon presents not only an image of God-likeness to the observer, but whether in that presentation it concurrently conveys a message that the human observer is called to respond to the iconic message by way of conformity to its central message. There is, consequently, no heteronomous legalistic character to the use of the term "normative" in this sense. "Normative" in this sense is endeictic and evocative of our true goal and purpose as human beings. Stating the goal of God-likeness thus bears with it an expectation of its fulfillment. It is in this sense that the normative character of icons is addressed in this paper.

The affirmation that the icon is the "book of the illiterate,"[25] in the words of St. John of Damascus, is but an aspect of the patristic affirmation of the icon as having didactic purpose. As a first step to showing the normative character of the icon it is important to emphasize the "humanward" movement of the icon. Much of the struggle against the iconoclastic movement was on the opposite side of the coin, that is, to show the icon's legitimate relationship to the divine. Just as the words of the Gospel instruct, so it is that for the sake of those who could not read, John of Damascus says in his "Exposition of the Orthodox Faith, "the Fathers gave their sanction to depicting these events on images as befit acts of great heroism, in order that they should form a concise memorial of them."[26] Thus, the 82nd canon of the 6th Ecumenical Council authorized the full human icon (and not symbolic representation of Christ as a lamb) "in order to expose to the sight of all, at least with the help of painting, that which is perfect..."[27]

Beyond this, however, there is a patristic teaching which points even more strongly to the normative purpose and character of the icon. That is, its purpose is not only to provide knowledge, nor only to point to higher realms, but it exists in order to provoke a response to that reality. It calls for a response of imitation, so to speak, that the painted icon causes the living icon of God to respond in life and behavior in imitation of Christ and the Saints whom the painted icon presents. Implicit is the living icon's essential human freedom to respond affirmatively or negatively to the ethical imperative of the icon.

Thus, Saint Basil, in his homily "On the Forty Holy Martyrs" makes the parallel between the persuasive function of rhetoric and the persuasive function of the painting: "The brave deeds accomplished in time of war are celebrated by both orators and artists. Orators remember them with decorous words; artists with paintbrush and canvas, and both inspire everyone with valor. That which words are to the ear, silent pictures reveal for imitation."[28] In his sermon on the martyr Barlaam, St. Basil gives us a personal experience of this impact of the icon. After comparing the feebleness of his own writing with the power of the icon in depicting the courage of the saint, he exclaims, "Would that I may be included in this image, and be united with Christ, the Judge of the contest. To Him be glory unto ages of ages!"[29]

Another defender of icons during the iconoclastic period, Patriarch Nikephoros of Constantinople also serves to point to the normative character of the icon. In his book, *In Defense of the Faith*, Fr. John Travis describes the theology of Nikephoros in reference to the iconographer's craft. Several reasons justifying its place in the worship of the Church are delineated. One is that "iconography as a craft has a divine purpose, our salvation and future blessedness." This is a concern with the human side of the theology of the icon, in that "it leads us to the evangelical vision and memory of those things characterized as honorable and venerable." Further, "iconography is functionally instructive," it is an "educational visual aid."[30] This is familiar territory.

But Nikephoros also moves on toward the normative dimension. For, Nikephoros writes, people, "by looking at the painted images, bring to mind the valiant deeds of those who served

God with all sincerity and (are thus) incited to rival the glorious and ever-memorable exploits, through which they exchanged earth for heaven…"[31] This still speaks of the icon, but sees it as a provocation for response by the faithful. While it exclusively describes those who favorably respond, not taking into account those who do not, it nevertheless presents the icon as bearing a message whose purpose it is to elicit a response.

It is St. John of Damascus who most clearly presents the normative dimension of the icon by articulating that one of its purposes is to elicit imitation of the one pictured in the icon by the one viewing it. He does this in several places. Regarding the saints, in his *Exposition of the Orthodox Faith*, he writes, "Let us raise monuments to them and visible images, and let us ourselves become, through imitation of their virtues, living monuments and images of them."[32] Elsewhere in the same work in his chapter "Concerning Images" he again refers to the emulation and imitation of the saints.[33]

However, the function of the icon to provoke imitation toward virtue is most clearly seen in St. John of Damascus' three homilies on the Divine Images. I would like to present this evidence in the form of an uncommented-upon *catenae* of excerpts from these writings so that they may make their own impact, reserving my comment for the conclusion of this section.

> (T)hings which have already taken place are remembered by means of images, whether for the purpose of inspiring wonder, or honor, or shame, or to encourage those who look upon them to practice good and avoid evil.[34]

> I bow down before the images of Christ, the incarnate God; of our Lady, the Theotokos and Mother of the Son of God; and of the saints, who are God's friends. In struggling against evil they have shed their blood; they have imitated Christ who shed His Blood for them by shedding their blood for Him. I make a record of the prowess and sufferings of those who have walked in His footsteps, that I may be sanctified, and be set on fire to imitate them zealously.[35]

Shame on you wicked devil, for grudging us the sight of our Master's likeness, and the holiness which proceeds from it...You are jealous of the honor which God has given to the saints. You wish us neither to see their glory portrayed nor zealously to imitate their courage and faith.[36]

But concerning this business of images, we must search for the truth, and the intention of those who make them. If it is really and truly for the glory of God and of His saints, to promote virtue, the avoidance of evil and the salvation of souls, then accept them with due honor...[37]

Images are a source of profit, help, and salvation for all, since they make things so obviously manifest, enabling us to perceive hidden things. Thus, we are encouraged to desire and imitate what is good and to shun and hate what is evil.[38]

The sixth kind of image is made for the remembrance of past events... They assist the increase of virtue that evil men might be put to shame and overthrown, and they benefit generations to come, that by gazing on such images we may be encouraged to flee evil and desire good.[39]

Therefore, we now set up images in remembrance of valiant men, that we may zealously desire to follow their example.[40]

Finally, let me note that St. John of Damascus, in the second of these homilies, instructs his readers that "the truth must be distinguished from falsehood in everything, and it is necessary to investigate whether the motive of each deed is good or bad."[41]

That quite ethical injunction is applicable, as well, to the concerns of this paper relating ethics to icons. The Damascene has clearly indicated to us through the passages just quoted that one of the purposes of a genuine icon is that it provoke choices for good and the avoidance of evil. One of the reasons icons are presented in worship is to impress the virtue of the person depicted upon us, to incite us to respond positively to it, and to incorporate it into our lives. It is this sense that one of the purposes of the icon is to produce a hunger for righteousness in us. This may have caused the 7th Ecumenical Council to include in its decree on the icons the teaching that frequent contemplation of icons lifts men up "to the memory of their prototypes, and to a longing after them."[42]

FORGETFULNESS AND RENEWAL OF THE TRADITION

If it be true then, that there is a normative dimension to the icon, thus creating a connection between the icon and ethics in the Eastern Christian tradition, why has this tradition by and large been forgotten in most of the theological writing about icons in the contemporary Orthodox Church? I believe that this might be explained by two major historical factors. These are, first, the course of the iconoclastic polemic and, second, by the distinction between Eastern Christian approaches to the icon and Western approaches to it.

The Iconoclastic Polemic

Jaroslav Pelikan, in his *The Spirit of Eastern Christendom*,[43] points to differing approaches to the theology of the icon from the perspective of the Orthodox iconophile tradition: the "traditional," the "christological," and the "scholastic." The major figures in the development of these approaches were John of Damascus, Theodore the Studite, and Patriarch Nikephoros of Constantinople, all of whom were directly involved in the iconoclastic controversy. Each responded in their defense to different kinds of challenges. For example, one can see that difference clearly in the quite "pastoral" tenor of the Damascene and the "philosophical/scholastic" tone of Theodore the Studite.

A careful reading of Theodore the Studite's three "Refutations of the Iconoclasts"[44] provides not one shred of evidence for concern from his perspective on what we have called here "the human side" of the icon. Rather, his concern is to deal with the philosophico-theological issues related to the religious legitimacy of the icon. In part, the placing of the issue exclusively on the "divine side" of the icon effectively robbed it of its normative emphasis. Much of the subsequent treatment of icons in Orthodox history tended to do the same thing. This was in concert with other factors as well. The conservative ethos forced on the Church by the Ottoman domination and policies of Peter the Great tended to turn the whole of worship and liturgy into a grand yet secret mystery play, which was focused more upon itself than upon the worshipper. The theological emphasis on the "icon in itself" was then the motif for subsequent response to Protestant iconoclastic charges. In it all, the aspect of the purpose of the icon designed to challenge response from the worshipper was lost.

Further, inasmuch as the Orthodox theology of the icon developed in the first instance as an apologetic and a defense against the attacks of the iconoclasts, it formulated its positions and arguments in opposition to theirs. It is oftentimes noted that the iconoclasts were not all of the same mind. While many sought the total destruction of the icons, others were willing to keep them provided they were placed high enough so that they could be seen, but not venerated.[45] Part of the Studite's argument against the iconoclasts precisely consisted in opposing this view.[46] The Studite thus reports the position of some of the iconoclasts: "...at another time they...say instead, that the depiction is good, because it is useful for education and memory, but is not for veneration. For this reason they assign the icon a place high up in the church..."[47] Could it be that precisely because this seemed to be an aspect of an iconoclast argument, that Theodore never wanted to assert it or appear to adopt it? Did this help create an environment which did not want to encourage an approach to the icon which focused on its human side, its normative aspect?

This, indeed, would seem to be the case, since there was a long-standing positive iconoclastic argument regarding the ethical aspect of icons. Milton V. Anastos, in his article "The Ethical Theory of Images Formulated by the Iconoclasts in 754 and 815"[48] documents this iconoclastic approach. This view argued against the icons as inadequate for ethical assistance, since it was the prototypes, i.e. Christ and the saints, who served this purpose through their lives, and not the "soul-less" (ἄψυχα) icons. In order to combat such a view, it was precisely the "God-ward" dimension of the icon which had to be affirmed and de-fended, that is, to show how the icon was precisely a "window on heaven" and a vehicle of communion with the divine. Focus on this aspect of the icon was necessary to combat not only the charge of idolatry, but also to provide the grounding for a de-fense of the "human-ward" side of the icon. In the process it is easy to understand how it may have been the required theologi-cal tactic not to speak of the "human-ward" side of the icon, so long as the "God-ward" side had not be accepted by the oppo-nents. In the further treatment, the historically conditioned "other-worldly dimensions" the Orthodox experience in the Turkish Ottoman Empire and in the Russia of Peter the Great may have served to blunt and almost eliminate the memory of the "humanward" and ethical dimensions of the icon.

The Western Approach

This argument might appear stronger for us if we observe another dynamic which characterized the Latin or Western part of the Church. There, historical forces can be seen as reinforc-ing the Eastern "God-ward" approach to the icon, and encour-aging an unwillingness to address the "human-ward," ethical aspect of the icon. Fr. Meyendorff points out that it was only the Byzantine Church that fully developed the theology of the icon. He notes: "Of all the cultural families of Christianity – the Latin, the Syrian, the Egyptian, or the Armenian – the Byz-antine was the only one in which art became inseparable from theology."[49]

The West's views of the icon were not anywhere as theologi-cally grounded as were those of the East, nor was iconography as widely developed. The concept of the sanctity of matter, so strongly emphasized in the East, had a much less central place in the thought and piety of the West. As J. M. Hussey put it, "This was a conception not unknown in the West (and found in writings ranging from St. Augustine to Teilhard de Chardin), but in general it was not so much emphasized by western modes of thought. This may be one reason why icons never played so powerful a role in Latin worship as in that of the Orthodox Churches, nor was deification generally so stressed in the West."[50]

Though the Latins accepted the 7th Ecumenical Council, the Franks and the Carolingians were not enthusiastic about icons. Charlemagne's code of laws, the *Libri Carolini*, emphasized that icons have only a representative character. According to Ernst Benz, this view "led to an essentially instructional and aesthetic concept of images" which focused primarily on them as educational means for the illiterate.[51] In the controversies between East and West following the Great Schism (11th century), the West's exclusive "human-ward" view may have provoked a greater focus, in the East, on the theological "divine side," of the icon, rather than on the "human side," as the conflicts between the two caused East and West to search for uniqueness and differentiation peculiar to their own positions.

As a result of these historical circumstances, it appears that the East tended more and more to forget the normative character of the icon as the years went by.

Reviving the Tradition

There has begun a reclaiming of the tradition of the normative character of the icon, however. The message is still hard to hear among the Orthodox, but credit must be given to Leonid Ouspensky for lifting this dimension up again for us. It seems as if many Eastern Orthodox still want to focus exclusively on the "divine" side of the icon, tending to continue to ignore the evidence for the normative side of the icon. That is why the message must be affirmed once again.

In the first instance, Ouspensky presents us with the icon's connection with the renewal of human nature as the icon of God. He writes:

Thus, holiness is the achievement of the possibilities given to man by the divine incarnation. It is an example to us. As for the icon, it portrays this achievement, it 'explains' it in an image. The icon is intimately connected with the renewal, the deification of the human nature realized by Christ.

Ouspensky takes us back to the "Synodicon" of the 7th Ecumenical Council, whose third paragraph honors those "who believe and who substantiate their words with writings and their deeds with representations, for the propagation and affirmation of the truth by words and images." He emphases the phrase "their deeds with representations," saying, "The presentations imply, therefore, that there are deeds which should be represented." These representations are of two closely related kinds. "On the one hand man can reestablish through the grace of the Holy Spirit his likeness to God. He can transform himself by an internal effort and make of himself a living icon of God." On the other hand, "man can also, for the good of others, translate his inner sanctification into images, either visible or verbal... Man can therefore also create an external icon, making use of matter which surrounds him and which has been sanctified by the coming of God on earth."[52] Thus, the central ethical act for the Orthodox faith, the active effort for the achievement of divinization, and the creation of the icon, "for the benefit of others," are presented by Ouspensky as having a common core whose essential purposes are identical. Ethics has become iconic; iconography has become normative.

As a result, the icon in Ouspensky's term becomes "a correct guide for our senses." The icon "is an important educational source. Herein," he says, "lies the essential goal of sacred art. Its constructive role does not lie only in the teaching of the truths of the Christian faith, but in the education of the entire man...The content of the icon is, therefore a true spiritual guide for Christian life and, in particular, for prayer."[53]

This normative dimension of the icon is thus, in Ouspensky's phrase "a path to follow" along with every other aspect of its rich reality. The goal of the icon "is to orient all of our feelings, as well as our intellect and all the other aspects of our nature, towards the transfiguration ... It works like the Gospel, to which it corresponds. Like the deification which it depicts, it suppresses nothing that is human, neither the psychological element, nor the diverse characteristics of man in the world."[54] The goal of the icon, its normative goal, is to speak to humanity so as to lead it to orient and direct human life "God-ward," toward divinization. The "human-ward" and the "God-ward" dimensions of the icon are intimately and essentially related.

ICON AND ETHICS

The Normative Message of the Icon

To this point in this paper we have sought to reclaim an earlier patristic tradition which perceived a "human side" to the icon. This aspect, which focused on the beholder of the icon, not only had the evocative power of art, but, we have contended, also presented to the beholder a normative challenge. In part, this occurred because of a natural confluence of the spirit of Orthodox ethics and Orthodox iconography. Insofar as he goes, Bulgakov is right when he characterizes Orthodox ethics as imbued with an aesthetic quality. He wrote that "the ideal foundation of Orthodoxy is not ethic, but religious, aesthetic; it is the vision of 'spiritual beauty;' to gain it one must have a 'spiritual art,' a creative inspiration."[55]

In this sense, both the icon and the Orthodox ethic share in the same aim, to present to the Christian the goal and *telos* of the life of all humanity and all creation, which is the transfiguration of all life and the cosmos toward the divine image. Both icon and ethics present before the observer, and in particular, the believing Christians, what the ultimate norm of human existence is: the deified humanity of Christ and the saints. Christians realize that norm as sanctified creatures.

Thus, Ouspensky clearly states, "...the icon represents the

human person, the bearer of a nature which has been deified and restored in its primitive purity. In other words, art, by its appropriate means, portrays the communion of this person with the divinity, his deification."[56] From the perspective of Orthodox ethics, "...the goal which embodies our proper humanity is directly commensurate with our beginning in God... We are to become as much as is humanly possible like God.... We become like God when our ways of thinking, feeling, acting and doing are united with God's way of doing things. We fulfill our purpose as human beings when we are thus united with God."[57]

But the icon has other normative characteristics as well. We can state some of them on what has been called by ethicists the "middle axiom" level, that is, not the ultimate norm which Orthodox ethics finds in God-likeness, nor on the level of the direct and immediate prescription or prohibition of concrete acts. The "middle axiom" level of ethical discourse provides general guidelines and principles for moral motives, intents, dispositions and actions.

Among several writers, Daniel J. Sahas has pointed to the fact that the icon by its very nature is contextualized in worship, an ecclesial and corporate phenomenon. "The icon cannot be understood apart from the wider cultural and theological context to which it belongs." He says:

> This context includes the character of the early Christian community, the essential distinctiveness of Christian theology from other perceptions of God... the value that Christianity bestows on humanity and on the material creation, the distinct faith in the incarnation of God and humanity's redemption and participation in the divine life, the theology of the Church in terms of her soteriological nature and liturgical character – to mention only a few aspects of this context. Apart from this theological context, or independent of any aspect of it, the icon becomes another painting, and obscure, unintelligible, or naive, for that matter.[58]

The icon, then, is an ecclesial, corporate phenomenon just as ethics is ecclesial and corporate, from the Orthodox Christian perspective. By its very nature the icon is communion uniting not only God and the believer who contemplates and reverences it, but also, its formal style and locus in the Church avoids any individualistic privatization of the icon. To reverence an icon is to affirm the commonly experienced truth and faith of the Church, it is an affirmation of our corporate reality as the body of Christ. Whatever else that means for Orthodox Christianity, it is also a normative standard by which selfishness, egotism and atomism are condemned as unfitting and inappropriate to Christian life; and by which community, mutual responsibility and love are affirmed.[59]

The very act of reverencing the icon (προσκύνησις) also has ethical import. The history of the Greek term is interesting because it is closely related to the relationship between subject and king. When the subject of the king offered προσκύνησις to him, it was an act of submissiveness, obedience, and an expression of personal commitment and loyalty, that is, a sign of an act of the will and an expression of an inner disposition.[60] Further, it was Byzantine practice to have this loyalty expressed by the subjects of the Emperor, whether he was present or not, through the reverencing of his representation. It is not necessary to document how the defenders of the icon used this royal practice to explain how the honor given to the icon is meaningful only insomuch as it is understood as being conveyed to the prototype. It is reminiscent of the liturgical "ought" repeated so frequently in the litanies of Orthodox worship, "let us commit ourselves and one another and our whole life to Christ our God."

This last observation leads a further elaboration of the corporate character of both the icon and ethics. We have noted a convergence of the range of "images of God" in the icon, including the human being as the "image of God." St. John of Damascus, together with other Fathers of the Church, holds to the opinion that humanity as a whole is the image of God. Honoring the icon of God, that is, respecting the inherent dignity of every human being, is thus a moral requirement. In fact,

St. John of Damascus sees this respect for the dignity of every human being precisely placed in our commonly shared image of God. He calls this respect for the dignity of each human being, "a relative worship" which is "our veneration of each other, since we are God's inheritance, and were made according to His image, and so we are subject to each other, thus fulfilling the law of love."[61] All Orthodox ethical discussion on human rights, and on justice issues, will eventually come back to this foundation. To reverence an icon is to affirm this commonly shared divine reality in every human being.

All of the theology of the icon regarding the acceptability of matter, and its sanctification, so frequently presented in the literature regarding the icon, also clearly provides "middle axiom" grounding for Orthodox ethical reflection on issues such as marriage, sex, economic justice, and ecology, to name only a few areas of contemporary concern. An example of this is approach is to be found in my article "The Integrity of Creation and Ethics" published in 1988.[62]

All of these finally coalesce in the understanding of the icon as an act of agapaic unity. It exists to unite the creature with the Creator; to relate the Savior with the redeemed; to elevate the believer to communion with God; to guide the community of the faithful to their ultimate goal; to reveal the beauty and majesty of the Church Triumphant to the Church Militant; to elicit commitment and reverence for God; to attract the believer into a communion with God as *theios eros*; to affirm the corporateness of the body of Christ; in short, (to slightly modify Sahas' phrase which was quoted earlier), the icon is an act of love by the Church, for the Church. It stands as an attractive, silent witness of God's love for humanity, pointing not to itself, but in both directions, heaven-ward and toward humanity. It is in this service that it offers itself. In itself, an icon is a response to the divine command that human beings "love God" with a full heart, mind, soul, and spirit, and that we love our neighbor as ourselves. The icon as a gift to both God and man is an act of love; and love is the supreme virtue in the ethical teaching of Christianity.

ICONS AS CONCRETE MEANS OF NORMATIVE INSTRUCTION

This final section will be brief. I wish to show in as concrete a way as possible the functioning of the icon in a normative mode. I wish to go beyond the patristic statements regarding the icon as encouraging Christians in their spiritual lives by providing heroic examples of saints and martyrs. Two examples of the more concrete connection of the icon with moral teaching follow here.

The first has to do with the theology of marriage. Throughout the history of Eastern Christianity, there has been an ongoing tension in which the monastic life has often been portrayed as "true," "full," "perfect," and "angelic" Christianity. Often the result of this approach has been to weaken the place of marriage in the Christian way of life, considering it as merely a conventional institution designed to facilitate the need of the human race to propagate the species. Some of these views have strong dualistic implications to them, a perspective repeatedly condemned in the canon law and anti-heretical literature of the Church.

In contrast to such a low estimate of Christian marriage is the tradition which sees Christian marriage as something much more than simply an ecclesial approval or blessing on this otherwise natural social institution. In the tradition of St. John Chrysostom, Christian marriage is approached as the means for the transfiguration of sexuality into an image of the Kingdom of God.[63] The virtues of monasticism (purity, poverty, and obedience) can be realized in ways appropriate to the unique and special calling of marriage, in what Paul Evdokimov called "Interiorized Monasticism."[64]

Such a view of marriage means that while some are called to the monastic or celibate life, the vast majority of Christians are called to the married life, there to live to the fullest the Christian goal of God-likeness, or *theosis*. In this sense, the sacramental nature of Christian marriage is a path toward the transfiguration of life. While the celibate or monastic path does have a

Plate 1 - George Filippakis, *Transfiguration*.

Plate 2 - George Filippakis, *Slaughter of the Innocents.*

practical superiority, in that it is simpler, less encumbered, and less fraught with complications, both the monastic and the married callings are equal as to their goal, which is divinization, i.e., conformity to the divine image.[65]

All this is presented in the traditional icon of the Transfiguration of Christ on Mount Tabor. In this icon (plate 1), the Christ figure is radiant in white robes as He stands on the craggy promontory of Tabor. On either side of Christ are two figures from the Old Testament who behold the event, as described in the Gospel accounts of the Transfiguration.[66] They both stand within the aura of the light of the Transfiguration. They both are bowed toward Christ in reverence. They both extend their hands in prayerful adoration. Elijah (Elias) the prophet is celibate. Moses is married. It does not make any difference. They both share in the transfigured life.

The second icon I wish to share with you as an example of the connection of iconography and ethics is a quite unusual work of the contemporary iconographer George Filippakis, of Woodbury, New York, who is also the artist who painted the icon of the Transfiguration in plate 1. Mr. Filippakis earns his living as an iconographer. His work is well-known in the United States for the iconography of church interiors as well as the production of panel icons. He is one of dozens of active iconographers at work in this country today.

Filippakis' work is very traditional. In the spirit of Orthodox iconography, he does not seek to "express himself" in his work, but he seeks to reveal the truth of Faith. His work, like that of all iconographers, seeks to be a window on heaven, to translate into the forms of ecclesial art visions of Kingdom life. Nevertheless, Filippakis has sought to present a "Kingdom message" of a distinctively ethical character in a work displayed publicly for the first time at the Clergy-Laity Congress of the Greek Orthodox Archdiocese held in Boston in July of 1988. Inspired on the one hand by the traditional icon of the "Slaughter of the Innocents" and by an obviously ethical concern in regard to the increased visibility of the abuse of children in our age, he created an icon with the scriptural passage, "As you did it not to one of the least of these, you did it not to me" (Matthew 25.45) as its theme (plate 2). The central figure is Christ, kneeling with his hands outstretched in a protecting stance. Gathered within his sphere of protection are seven children. But beyond the limits of his hands are a series of five figures. On the left bottom, a woman in red holds out the arm of a child on her lap, while next to her a man directs a syringe toward the arm with one hand, while he pulls at the hair of another child. Clockwise, another man holds a child in his one arm while pointing a flagon of alcohol toward the child's mouth. The fourth figure, a man, stands to the right of Christ and holds a child hanging by its feet in one hand, while brandishing a long knife in its direction. The fifth figure is a woman with a child turned over on her knee as she raises above the child in her outstretched hand a multi-stringed whip. Three children lay dead at her feet. In the background is a crucified figure, not Christ, but a child. On the ground at the right knee of Jesus is a scroll indicating that the icon was painted in conjunction with the Archdiocesan emphasis on "The Year of the Homeless and Abused Children."

The icon is not just a picture. It is an icon. It reveals the divine condemnation of those who abuse children, whether through drugs or alcohol or killing or other violence. It also expresses the divine compassion for the suffering of these innocents. In all, however, it also clearly bears a normative message in regard to a scourge of our time, child abuse. As such it also has a "human-ward" message, a clear command regarding the behavior of Christians in regard to children who are threatened or are suffering abuse.

This icon, while far from typical, serves to highlight the ethical dimension of the icon.

CONCLUSION

This paper has sought to present a little-developed aspect of Eastern Christian iconography, its ethical dimension. The claim is that it has shown that one aspect of Orthodox iconography is normative, in its "human-ward" side. Consequently, it is a call for the restoration of this dimension of iconography to its teaching mission, but also to an expansion of the perceptivity of observers and communicants of icons to search for and perceive and share in the ethical dimensions of iconography.

ENDNOTES

*Published in *Orthodoxes Forum: Zeitschrift des Instituts für Orthodoxe Theologie der Universität München.* Vol. 4, 1990, no. 2, pp. 195-214.
[1]A first draft of this paper was read at the Annual Meeting of the Orthodox Theological Society in America, May 28-30, 1987. A number of the suggestions made by my colleagues at that time have been incorporated in this revision. This form of the paper was presented at the January 1989 Annual Meeting of the Society of Christian Ethics,

which met at Notre Dame.

[2]These quite elementary descriptions are drawn primarily from the account in Timothy Ware's *The Orthodox Church*. New York: Penguin Books, 1981, pp. 38-40, to which the reader is referred for more details as background to this paper.

[3]Ibid., p. 38.

[4]Stanley S. Harakas, *Toward Transfigured Life: The Theoria of Eastern Orthodox Ethics*. Minneapolis: Light & Life Publishing Co., 1983, ch. 1.

[5]Ibid., ch. 2.

[6]Vladimir Lossky, *Orthodox Theology: An Introduction*. Crestwood, NY: St. Vladimir's Seminary Press, 1978, pp. 71-72.

[7]Vladimir Lossky, *In the Image and Likeness of God*. Eds. John H. Erickson and Thomas E. Bird. Crestwood, NY: St. Vladimir's Seminary Press, 1974, p. 224.

[8]See Sergius Bulgakov, *The Orthodox Church*. Hialeah, FL: Orthodox Book Center, 1935, p. 179, and Stanley S. Harakas, op. cit., pp. 136-141.

[9]For various treatments of the icon in its historical and theological contexts, see, in the order of increasing complexity and depth, the following representative works: Ernst Benz, *The Eastern Orthodox Church*. Garden City, NY: Doubleday & Co., 1963, ch. 1; Manolis Chatzidakis & André Grabar, *Byzantine and Early Medieval Painting*. Trans. Simon Watson Taylor. New York: Viking Press, 1965. Nicholas V. Lossky, "The Significance of Second Nicaea," *Greek Orthodox Theological Review*, vol. 32, no. 4, 1987, pp. 335-340; Robert M. Arida, "Second Nicaea: The Vision of the New Man and New Creation in the Orthodox Icon." Ibid., pp. 417-424; Boris Bobrinskoy, "The Icon: Sacrament of the Kingdom." *St. Vladimir's Theological Quarterly*, vol. 31, no. 4, 1987, pp. 287-296. Nicholas Ozolin, "The Theology of the Icon." Ibid., pp. 297-308; Leonid Ouspensky, "Iconography of the Descent of the Holy Spirit." Ibid., pp. 309-348; Daniel J. Sahas, *Icon and Logos: Sources in Eighth-Century Iconoclasm*. Toronto: University of Toronto Press, 1986; Constantine D. Kalokyris, *The Essence of Orthodox Iconography*. Brookline, MA: Holy Cross Orthodox Press, 1985; Leonid Ouspensky, *Theology of the Icon*. Trans. Elizabeth Meyendorff. Crestwood, NY, 1978.

[10]*Theology and the Church*. Crestwood, NY: St. Vladimir's Seminary

Press, 1980, ch. IV.

[11]Op. cit., p. 138.

[12]Op. cit., p. 138.

[13]Ibid., p. 150.

[14]Ibid., pp. 40-41.

[15]Ibid., p. 42.

[16]Sahas, op. cit., pp. 12,13.

[17]Ibid., p. 10.

[18]Ibid.

[19]Op. cit., pp. 15-16.

[20] Ὀρθόδοξη Πνευματική Ζωή. Thessalonike: Pournaras, 1986, p. 30.

[21]Mantzarides, Χριστιανική Ἠθική. *2nd Ed.* Thessalonike: Pournaras, 1983, p. 170. Quoting St. Basil, Epistle 1, 3, Ed. Y. Courtonne, vol. 1, Paris, 1987, p. 8.

[22]Ibid.

[23]*In the Image and Likeness of God.* New York: St. Vladimir's Seminary Press, 1974, ch. 7.

[24]Ibid., p. 126.

[25]St. John of Damascus, *On the Divine Images: Three Apologies Against Those who Attack the Divine Images.* Trans. David Anderson. Crestwood, NY: St. Vladimir's Seminary Press, 1980, p. 28.

[26]Chapter XVI, *The Nicene and Ante-Nicene Fathers.* Second Series. Vol. IX.

[27]Quoted in John Meyendorff, *Byzantine Theology.* New York: Fordham University Press, 1974, p. 45

[28]Quoted by John of Damascus, op. cit., p. 91.

[29]Ibid., pp. 35-36.

[30]John Travis, *In Defense of the Faith: The Theology of Patriarch Nikephoros of Constantinople.* Brookline, MA: Holy Cross Orthodox Press, 1984, p. 48.

[31]Ibid., p. 58, note 25.

[32]Chapter XV, *Nicene and Ante-Nicene Fathers.* 2nd Series, Vol IX, p. 87.

[33]Ibid., Ch. XVI, p. 38.

[34]John of Damascus, *On Divine Images*, op. cit., 1, 13, p. 21.

[35]Ibid., 1, 21, p. 29. Translation slightly modified.

[36]Ibid., 2, 6, p. 53. Translation slightly modified.

[37]Ibid., 2, 21, p. 58.

[38]Ibid., 3, 17, p. 74.

[39]Ibid., 3, 23, p. 77.

[40]Ibid., 3, 23, p. 78.

[41]Ibid., 2, 10, p. 57.

[42]*Nicene and Post-Nicene Fathers*, 2nd Series, vol. XIV, p. 550.

[43]Chicago: University of Chicago Press, 1974, pp. 119.

[44]St. Theodore The Studite, *On the Holy Icons*. Trans. Catharine P. Roth. Crestwood, NY: St. Vladimir's Seminary Press, 1981.

[45]Jaroslav Pelikan. Ibid., pp. 130-133.

[46]"1st Refutation," 13. On the Holy Icons, ibid, p. 34.

[47]"2nd Refutation of the Iconoclasts," Introduction. Ibid., p. 43.

[48]*Dumbarton Oaks Papers: Number Eight*. Cambridge, MA: Harvard University Press, 1954, pp. 152-160.

[49]Op. cit., p. 52.

[50]J. M. Hussey, *The Orthodox Church in the Byzantine Empire*, Oxford: Clarendon Press, 1986, p. 68.

[51]Ernst W. Benz, "Christian Doctrine," *Encyclopedia Britannica*, vol. 16, pp. 372-3.

[52]Ouspensky, *The Theology of the Icon.*, ibid., p. 192.

[53]Ibid., p. 210.

[54]Ibid., p. 211.

[55]Sergius Bulgakov, *The Orthodox Church*. Hialeah, FL: Orthodox Book Center, 1935, p. 179.

[56]Ibid., p. 214.

[57]Stanley S. Harakas, *Toward Transfigured Life*. Minneapolis, MN: Light and Life Publishing Co., 1983, p. 28.

[58]Sahas, op.cit., p. 5. My emphasis.

[59]See also, George Mantzarides, ibid. for a fuller development of this ethical perspective, p. 34 ff.

[60]Demetrios Constantinides, "Προσκύνησις" in Θρησκευτικὴ καὶ Ἠθικὴ Ἐγκυκλοπαίδεια, v. 10, pp. 656-657.

[61]John of Damascus, *On the Divine Images*, 3, 37, op. cit., p. 87. For a similar statement by Cyril of Jerusalem, see p. 102.

[62]*St. Vladimir's Theological Quarterly*, vol. 32, no. 1, 1988, pp. 27-42.

[63]St. John Chrysostom *On Marriage*. Crestwood, NY: St. Vladimir's Seminary Press, 1986.

[64]*The Struggle With God*. Tr. Sister Gertrude. New York: Paulist Press,

1966, Ch. 7, pp. 111-130. See also Vincent Rossi, "Sanctity, Sexuality and Sacrifice," *Epiphany*, Winter, 1987, pp. 30-34.
[65]Stephen Muratore, "The Nobler Calling: Marriage or Monasticism?" *Epiphany*, Winter, 1987, pp. 53-55.
[66]Matthew 17 and Mark 9.

9

A Case Study in Eastern Orthodox Ethics on Rich and Poor: Alexios Makrembolites' "Dialogue Between the Rich and the Poor"

Alexios Makrembolites, a fourteenth century Eastern Orthodox Christian, wrote an interesting essay on relations between economic classes entitled, "Dialogue Between the Rich and the Poor."[1]

The purpose of this paper is to view this writing from the perspective of Christian ethics, to analyze its content and argumentation from an ethical perspective, and to offer an evaluation regarding its place within the framework of Eastern Orthodox thought, with a few ideas about its contemporary meaning. In order to do this, some background material indicating the sociopolitical context will be presented.

Consequently, I propose to divide the body of this paper into the following sections: the sociopolitical context; Makrembolites as moralist; the ethical argument of the "Dialogue," and the derivation of Makrembolites' ethics. In the conclusion, I will suggest some contemporary implications of this work.

The Sociopolitical Context

The "Dialogue" was written sometime between October and November of 1343 in Constantinople. The political situation in Byzantium at that time was one of general decline, turmoil, civil wars, and perhaps open class conflict. The history of this period is a history of the Byzantine Empire in dissolution. Taking place during the Paleologian dynasty – the last of Byzantium – it saw the Empire beleaguered on all sides: Western European forces and Germanic advances from the north and Turkish military progress from the east.

The Greeks recovered Constantinople in 1261, following the Latin occupation, which arose out of the Fourth Crusade in 1204. But Byzantium's power was broken and its economic strength vitiated by both internal and external forces. Economic concessions had been given over to the rising commercial powers of Italian republics such as Venice and Genoa, including critical rights extracted after the traders of Genoa imposed their will in a victorious war over the imperial forces.

Internally, long-developing socio-economic trends had reached a crisis point. In terms of political conflict, the imperial center was at odds with the great landowning magnates. These had received their power originally as grants to farmer-soldiers on the empire's borders. Little by little they displaced the peasants, or made them *paroikous* (πάροικους, serfs) and created extensive fiefdoms of such military and economic independence that imperial power to wage war and to levy taxes was severely reduced. Consequently, it was imperial policy in general to support the interests of the lower classes of small farmers, artisans, small entrepreneurs, sailors, and workers against the large landowners; that is, the poor against the rich. Between the two was the middle class, "to whom belonged merchants, manufacturers, rich craftsmen, small landowners, and professional men."[2] Below the "poor class" of small farmers, laborers, artisans, and small storekeepers were the destitute poor, who stood at the one extreme of the class spectrum, countered by the very rich landowning magnates on the other extreme.

At this crucial time in the dying days of the Empire, a civil war broke out between an elderly retired Emperor, Andronikos II, and his profligate grandson, Andronikos III. The younger Emperor, in seeking support to stay in power, came into an alliance with an ambitious rebellious leader in the almost independent region around Thessalonike, John Kantakouzenos. In the early stages of his rise to power, Kantakouzenos had attracted the support of the farmer/artisan poor, but he soon alienated them when he sided with the noble upper class. When he was proclaimed emperor in the area of Thrace, it triggered a successful counter-revolution of the small farmer and artisan class. These revolutionaries became known in history as "the Zealots." The Zealot revolutionaries attacked, massacred, and expelled many of the aristocratic families of Thessalonike, and established a government there which "in certain respects resembled a real republic."[3] This event took place three years after the writing of the "Dialogue" which we are studying.

In seeking to understand the socio-political context of Makrembolites' "Dialogue" it is, therefore, important to note that it was no longer a struggle of the ambitions of two persons who contested with each other for the supreme power. Rather, it was a struggle between two classes, of which one wanted to maintain its privileges and the other attempted to throw off its yoke.[4]

Demetrios Kydones, a contemporary, opined that Thessalonike was regarded as the teacher of the other cities "in the uprisings of the populace against the aristocracy."[5]

MAKREMBOLITES AS MORALIST

It was in these times that Alexios Makrembolites lived, worked, and wrote. He was not very much noticed by his contemporaries or by modern scholarship until less than a century ago. The only manuscript containing his twelve short extant writings belongs historically to the patriarchal Library of Jerusalem,[6] which was described bibliographically just ninety years ago for the first time.[7]

Makrembolites was a representative of the lower level of intellectuals living in Constantinople at the time. He appears to have done civil service work and to have been a teacher. He is not widely read in the classics, but does know Scripture well.

His concerns are not primarily theoretical, but rather, his writings show a deep involvement with the problems and social realities of his contemporaries, which by and large he seeks to address from his Christian perspective. His writing is at times guarded, with an eye to the current political forces swirling about him. He lived during the civil war of Andronikos II and Andronikos III, which was won by the latter with the help of John Kantakouzenos. He lived in Constantinople. His sympathies surely were with the cause of the grandfather, who espoused the policy of imperial support of the lower classes against the upper classes. However, it was not politic to be too outspoken when the younger Andronikos and Kantakouzenos had aligned themselves with the nobility and seemed to have the upper hand in Constantinople. As one would expect, the Zealots of Thessalonike supported the elder Andronikos in the civil war. But as we shall see, Makrembolites was a spokesman not for the poorest of the poor against the nobles, but the increasingly impoverished lower middle class against the upper-middle *bourgeoisie* merchant class.

If this is the case, are we entitled to think of Makrembolites as anything more than as a propagandist? Certainly, he is not an academic ethicist interested in the subtleties of theory and disinterested in the application of ethics to practical circumstances. Yet the range of his twelve extant writings shows that he was not a one-issue writer, and that he conceived of the topics he wrote about in moral categories. His extant writings are nearly all in the form of "Λόγοι," or homilies, and appear to be dominated by patterns of thought which evidence a moralist's mind.

This becomes evident with a simple renearsal of some of the topics of Makrembolites' literary corpus. These are found in the *Sabbaiticus* 417 manuscript, and I mention some of them so as to establish his interest in moral questions.[8]

Document 1: A defense of the married life in the light of the strong monastic values in Byzantine society. It is an attempt to prove that true renunciation of evil (ἀπόταξις) is dependent upon the inner dispositions (προαίρεσιν) and not upon mere obedience to law. He seeks to show that there are other ways to achieve spiritual and moral purity comparable to the monastic life, and that not only the celibate may be saved but the married as well, "for evil comes not from the material world, but from our will and inner disposition (γνώμης καὶ προαιρέσεως)." He appeals to scriptural precedent and early church history by arguing that monks are not the only ones to be saved, since the saving work of Christ took place long before monasticism had been established *Logos 1* takes up thirteen and one-half folio pages.

Document 2: A "proof" that the successes of the Mohammedans were due to the sins of the Byzantines. Makrembolites holds that it is impossible to be saved through a nominal Christian faith only, just as it is impossible to live without breathing, for faith without works is dead, as are works without faith. In spite of this, the Mohammedan's faith is not true and those among the Christians who support such a position are in error. *Logos 2* consists of thirty folio pages.

Document 4: A dialogue on faith and unfaith, a polemical tract against Islam. This work once again returns to the problem of theodicy in the context of the reverses of the Christians before the Moslem faith, "posed by the thriving of the godless." *Logos 4* is thirteen and one-half folio pages long.

Document 5: The fifth *Logos* in the manuscript is the "Dialogue Between the Rich and the Poor," the subject matter of this paper. It takes up thirteen and one-half folio pages.

Document 6: Entitled "Concerning 'What is Hell?'" *Logos 6* is eleven folio pages long and presents a form of the meonic understanding of evil, for Makrembolites teaches that Hell is the absence of the knowledge of God.

Document 7: This writing is seven folio pages long, an unnumbered *Logos* "On God's justice." It is addressed to a priest about to lose his faith in God's justice on account of poverty. It is people entrusted with the conduct of affairs, not God, who are unjust, Makrembolites argues. This writing is short, only one folio page long.

Document 8: *Logos 8* is entitled, "From where Health and Sickness?" a study which may have been prompted by the beginnings of the plague of 1347. Makrembolites argues that both health and sickness have their source in God, theologically speaking. Concurrently, he holds that from a physical point of view the balance of all the elements of the body insure health, and their imbalance causes sickness, a wholistic approach to human well-being. There follows a short "complaint" which "bemoans bad times, wars, captivity, and atrocities." The whole covers three and one-half folio pages.

Document 9: The next writing is in fact a hymnological canon. It is written as "a proof that love stands above all the virtues." From a marginal note it appears to have been written at the very height of the civil war between the two Andronikos'. Beginning with the words "Peace, both sure and God-granted," it teaches that a truly reverent person "should avoid violent struggle and pillage and choose love instead." Interestingly, the acrostic of this hymn, a frequent Byzantine literary device, is "I love peace. God's admirable favor." It certainly is a call for peace in the midst of revolutionary times, but probably not a pacifist statement.

Document 14: *Logos 9* is a writing against the Genoese, who are presented as being two-faced recipients of Byzantine benificences who maliciously turned on their benefactors and who provoked a war against their benefactors through insidious plots. It is about fourteen folio pages long.

One last bibliographic note. Three of his works have been published: an allegory on Lucian, the treatment of the Genoese war, and the dialogue between the rich and the poor. In addition, some of Makrembolites' scattered epigrams have been published.[10]

The repetition of this list serves quite adequately to indicate the concerns of Makrembolites and to clearly stamp him as a writer interested in moral issues and motivated by a strong moral sense, as will become clear in the following section. Though Makrembolites could not have been an ethicist in the modern sense of the word, he was a moralist, approaching numerous topics with both the interest in the betterment and salvation of his hearers[1] but also with a definite perception of those topics cast in ethical categories. The "Dialogue" which we are about to analyze for its ethical arguments is a clear case in point.

THE ETHICAL ARGUMENTS OF THE "DIALOGUE"

In spite of the implications of the title, the "Dialogue" is not an easy exercise of confrontation between the impoverished poor and the landowning magnates of Byzantine society. Rather, it pits the class of artisans, peasants, small farmers and others, who, because of the declining fortunes of the Empire, are suffering serious reverses against the still prospering upper middle class.[11] I begin this treatment by quoting a few passages from the "charge" of the Poor against the Rich, not only in order to set the stage for the actual eleven-part dialogic exchange which follows, but also to give a sense of the tenor of the "dialogue."[12] A word of caution is necessary for the 20th century reader of these lines. In spite of the fact that Makrembolites uses uncharacteristically strong and direct language in the "Dialogue," his intents are ameliorative, not revolutionary. He wants a "humanizing" of the class structures, not their abolishment. The strength of the rhetoric should not mislead the reader in misinterpreting the intent of the author.

The Charge of the "Poor" Against the "Rich"

How long will we bear your greediness, O Brothers, who are not brothers in your attitude? How long will the Father common to us all be magnanimous, seeing you appropriate common goods to yourselves? How long will He abstain from wrath, from shaking the earth, beholding us to give up the ghost in want and you own, beyond necessity, possessions which you bury beneath the earth? But she, the common mother, will not accept them at all. She quakes, and rightly so, eager to swallow up those who act in such a way: for although she has no soul, she does not wish to receive back and keep what once has issued from her belly: she wishes that it be sent to other stomachs – namely ours.

These possessions have been given for us all to use... How then can you wish to be the sole proprietors of such things as are composed of these? Do you not see how quickly they change possessors and then how easily once more fall into others hands? Thank God! For were you able to seize the sun, you would prevent our enjoying its rays![14]

How can you abuse the possessions of our common Father or rather ours, and not be ashamed? Were you superior to us in virtue, all right, but even then it would not be just, for those whose deeds are virtuous should imitate God's equity. But if you are not, how is it that you do not quake at the thought of our common Father's everlasting wrath? For the accusation of the sin against nature which weighs upon you is coupled with that of your not heeding your brethren when their life and death lie in your hands.

...It is for this reason, that we are so much wasted by envy, sinful though it be, whenever we see you, possessors of many goods, quite unmoved by our indigence. Not even by the smallest of gifts do you hasten to quench the furnace of poverty in which we burn, though anything would suffice for us.

Are you not shamed to hear how the gentiles treat the poor ones of their kin or their prisoners of war from among us? Why do they not consider any one of the unworthy of due care? It is the height of unreasonableness that Jews and Mohammedans should be humane and merciful while the disciples of Christ, who was by nature humane and merciful should be heartless and niggardly towards their kin. It is to us that you owe the goods of this world, and only those amongst you who have mercy toward us will partake in the rewards of the future life.

Some of the major ethical themes in the subsequent portions of the dialogue are revealed in these selected passages of the "Charge." The whole situation is cast in terms of the vice of greed over which it is assumed that the "Rich" have moral control, and can change if they wish. The arguments of the "Dialogue" placed in the exhortations of the "Poor" are designed in their totality to support the position that the "Rich" *ought* to become more merciful and philanthropic in their inner dispositions and in their deeds. From this perspective, it is clearly a treatise strongly ethical in purpose and character.

Throughout the "Dialogue" there is a broad-based arsenal of appeals that presuppose a set of ethical assumptions that include nearly all of the traditional and standard schools of ethical thought. Chief among these is the assumption that ethical reflection and behavior are inseparable from our relationship with God. Of almost equal significance, however, is an appeal to the nature of created reality, a sort of loose and ready natural law approach. From the manner of argumentation and the contexts of the argument, it is obvious that Makrembolites distinguishes between the two, while understanding them to be compatible with each other. In addition, throughout the "Dialogue" he uses a consequence approach to the morality of the situation. For example, persistence in the heartless approach by the "Rich" will insure their eternal condemnation, A theological hedonism, however, guarantees bliss and happiness in this life as well as in the life to come for those who show mercy upon the "Poor." No less evident is a strong thread of *Theosis* ethics, particularly in the assumption that human beings are called to function in a God-like manner, in imitation of God's own caring, love, and philanthropy.

Three other themes of Eastern Orthodox Christian ethics also appear in the "Charge." One of the strong traits of Eastern Christianity is its tendency to use shame as a motivating force to bring about change in behavior, rather than guilt, understood in a juridical sense. Shame as a sanction is used frequently throughout this work. Further, the "Charge" presents an interesting teleological approach to wealth. The purpose of wealth is to destroy poverty and it is not "wealth," properly so called, unless it serves this purpose. In a paragraph not quoted above,

Makrembolites uses a number of examples to prove his point.

> One would not call "rose" a flower which, though it deceives by its appearance, does not excel to some extent by the scent peculiar to it, nor "wine," that which does not inebriate us, nor "bread," a thing which does not quicken the stomach, nor "fire," that which does not burn, nor "water," that which does not cool and quench the thirst – likewise, we speak not of "wealth" which does not feed the poor.[17]

Also present in the "Charge" Against the 'Rich'" as well as in several other places throughout the "Dialogue," is the theme of the fundamental common ownership (κοινοκτημοσύνη) of all material goods, which serves Makrembolites as the lynchpin for his argumentation on behalf of economic justice.

An Economic Argument: In response to the "Charge" that has been made against the "Rich," Makrembolites presents them as first singling out the economic issue, and defending themselves on the basis of this criterion. They are presented as responding that they really have no obligation to provide for those who do not provide any services to them. It is characteristic of Eastern Christian ethical thinking that the argument is not cast in juridical or legal terms but rather in terms of what is fitting and appropriate: "But it is not fitting that we feed for nothing those who do not serve us."[18]

The "Poor" counter that in refusing philanthropy to the needy, the "Rich" fail to serve God and evince a disdain for the poor, for which pride God will cause them to suffer eternal punishment. The response is then extended by an appeal to the injustice of the situation in that the "Poor" work hard and gain little, while the "Rich" work little, but gain much. This leads to another rebuttal of the economic objection that is based on the common humanity of both "Rich" and "Poor." This common humanity is defined as their shared reasoning ability, discernment of good and evil, dominion over creation, and the privilege and ability to pray. It is an appeal to commonly shared moral capacities, signifying that economic questions are not to be perceived autonomously and that they are in fact subject to moral considerations.

The "Rich" then seek a clarification. They want to know how precisely their stance does injury and harm to the human dignity of the "Poor." The response of the "Poor" is cast in terms of conflicting values. The "Rich" denigrate the humanity of the "Poor" "by preferring corporal to spiritual values."[19]

Appeal to Determinism: As if to extend the first objection by the "Rich," Makrembolites places in their mouths an argument of economic determinism: "It is in the nature of things that you should always fare ill and suffer evil while we are everywhere successful."[20] Put in contemporary terms, the argument is that the rich are rich precisely because of their inherent superior qualities, while the poor are poor precisely because they do not have the inherent capacities to be wealthy. The "Poor" counter this form of economic determinism argument with a brief response based on the coherence of reason and morality, "for," they say, "if such were the case, all the rich would be good, having their riches from God, and the poor, (would be) bad, being destitute of God. But this is not so, not at all so."[21] Rather, the "Poor" attribute their penury not to nature, but to circumstances. Makrembolites numbers the various ways wealth is both gained and lost: knowledge, trade, abstinence, rapine, domination, and inheritance. On this basis, an appeal is made for sharing. When the "Rich" offer an argument purporting to appeal to an "organic principle" of the whole having dominion over the parts, that is, another attempt to support a justification of their wealth based on nature, the "Poor" respond with a straightforward appeal to justice and fairness, based on the same organic argument, but appealing to the consequences:

> Do you not see what happens when an element claims more than its fair portion and tries to seize the place of others? Does it not destroy, in addition to its own sphere, that which it has usurped and cause the perdition of the living being?[22]

The "Poor" do not reject a corporate/organic dimension to the question, but they recognize that this approach cannot legitimately serve to justify the moral equivalent of cancer.

The "Poor" then press the argument by berating the extremely sharp social and class distinctions of the time, which not only prohibited intermarriage between the classes but even the sharing of meals together or even common conversation. This is wrong, it is held, because it is in contrast with the behavior of the Son of God who "consorted with the humble and considered it to be His glory, not a dishonor."[23] Significant for our study is the fact that this appeal to Christ as the prototype for human behavior is related in the same response to the view that "man, as much as he is able, resembles God."[24] This is a clear use of the *Theosis* perspective in the ethics of the poor.

The point is then hammered home by outlining the beneficial consequences which would occur if all these social discriminations were abolished. Intermarriages would eliminate poverty by sharing the wealth. "Through such a practice would poverty disappear, for it abounds in life for no other reason, I think, than that of like mating with like," he argues. Here we find not only a recognition of the moral implications of social structures, but even the intimation of an approach which would seek to correct social evils, through structural change rather than by individual moral endeavor. It is an idea that does not find too much resonance in the rest of this document.

The consequences of such an arrangement will be good. Both sides will benefit from such inter-relatedness. The "Poor" will achieve a measure of sustenance and the "Rich" not only will avoid eternal torments, but will in fact feed Christ as they feed the poor. In doing this they will not diminish their greatness but enhance it, for they then act as persons given a trust for the benefit of others,

The appeal is to "respect our common nature,"[25] but there is no expectation of absolute equality: Makrembolites is no egalitarian. "May luxury be your share and *sustenance* ours. . . . Let *everything* of yours be for luxury: of ours, for the satisfaction of our wants and bodily needs."[26]

But the commonality of the "Rich" and the "Poor" is still affirmed: "We differ from you in substance, not nature,"[27] Further, the appeal to consequences is not only applied to the afterlife of the "Rich." They should support the "Poor" because even in this existence they need these "Poor" for their own well-being; that is, "the tillers of the soil, the builders of houses and merchant ships and the craftsmen."[28]

Makrembolites thus demolished with a series of rebuttals the argument of the "Rich" that riches and poverty are determined by nature, anticipating by five hundred and fifty years the debate surrounding contemporary theories of sociobiology.

Escaping the Categories: The "Rich" are then portrayed as shifting the ground of the debate. They are presented as conceding that the arguments so far raised by the "Poor" may in fact apply to the "extremes" on the economic spectrum, but that they are of neither – they are the "μέσοι," the middle class. Yet even here they retain a measure of their economic determinism, for they claim that it is from the two, the extreme of poverty and the extreme of wealth, that moral evils such as "theft, drunkenness, laxity, slander, envy and murder take their origin."[29] They are not to be ascribed to the middle class. The "Poor" sidestep the argument but agree that neither extreme has ever been of any help to them, leaving the "μέσοι" as the only ones the "Poor" can appeal to for assistance.

There then follows a series of characteristically "middle class" arguments by the "Rich" of the dialogue seeking on quite self-serving grounds to justify their refusal to aid the "Poor." Paradoxically, the "Poor" make an appeal to Providence, that God will provide for their children, "as He provided for (theirs),"[30] so it is not necessary for them to plan for the future. This biblical perspective, however, is quickly turned into a convoluted consequence argument: "How will the Father of the spirits care for your children when they become the cause of the indigence of others?"[31] they ask.

Yet stringency in the application of the dominical requirements seems not to be what the "Poor" are actually demanding. All they are asking is for payment of wages due them for their work. It is merely a "just wages" appeal for them and the avoidance of extravagance in regard to the children of the "Rich," cast in a rather self-serving utilitarian framework.

> For the sake of your own spiritual salvation why do you not grant for our labors the portion which by law is ours? … Because of excessive gifts bestowed upon your[31] children, you are submitted to pitiless punishment.[32]

Undaunted by such reasonings, the "Rich" counter with another prudential argument: they can't give to the "Poor" because they need their wealth for their old age. In addition to a repetition of the need for trust in God's providence, the "Rich" introduce two additional arguments. The first moves the consequences of hardheartedness to a this-worldly assessment of the spiritual condition of the "Rich." For this way of thinking "deprives the soul of any hope of God, … it weakens faith and diminishes God's bounty."[33]

More ethically interesting is the response that counters this age-old "old age" concern, with a very powerful instrumentalist argument which holds that human beings are God's agents for the help of the "Poor." It is conceded that if God wanted to, He could readily feed the "Poor." But precisely in this situation Makrembolites has the "Poor" challenge the "Rich" with a spiritual and moral obligation of extremely commanding dimensions. He has the "Poor" say to the "Rich": "He is putting your discernment and obedience to the test and because of you deprives us of the very necessities of life, that you may gain Salvation through mercy on us."

The middle class rationale, however, reaches its moral nadir when it repeats what seems to be the perennial argument when all other defenses have been thrown down: the "Poor," they charge, are not really in need. Their pretended poverty is only a cover for their greed! And, of course, they add with solicitude, this gives the really poor and deserving a bad name.

Makrembolites' response is interesting. He does not deny subterfuge on the part of some of the "Poor," but rather notes that "they would not have contrived these things harmful to their lives, had you been prone to charity."[34] The retort continues with the contention that, regardless, the "Rich" are still subject to the commandments. They are to "follow the divine example," to avoid such "superfluous" and "inquisitive thought." In addition, the response appeals to the requirements that "bids you love us as yourself."

Of interest here, ethically, is the progression from commandment, to imitation of the divine example, to a focus on the inner dispositions, to a call to selfless love. The appeals follow one upon the other, supporting the view about Eastern Christian ethics that it does not contrast rule ethics, teleological ethics, formal (inner, dispositional ethics) and agapaic ethics, but rather sees them as parts of the total moral obligation.

Ethical Determinism and Self-determination: The "Rich" then seek to turn the tables as to who should be the object of such moral solicitude. "Why, then," Makrembolites has them say, "are you not moved by *our* misfortune?"[35] Their "misfortunes" consist of a litany of quite familiar complaints: too much government involvement in their affairs, having to deal with "the intrigues and denigrations of our peers" and the "crawling envy" for those who are more successful, and the anxiety needed to maintain it. Pleasure and happiness, they confess, come not from luxurious living "but in having a soul free from preoccupation."[36] This appeal to stoic dispassion does not have a very authentic ring to it. One would have expected a strong retort.

It is interesting, however, that this admission, which supports the views previously articulated by the poor, that the materialist outlook has evil consequences in this life as well as the next, received no comment from the "Poor." Perhaps it is because the "Rich" are then presented by Makrembolites as quickly reversing field and attacking the "Poor" with an all-too-familiar charge: the majority of the poor have chosen poverty on account of their meanness. At heart, this is a repetition of the nature argument. The "choice" which they make is not a free and open decision. It is produced by the conditions of their nature. A sort of Skinnerian behaviorist determinism is at the heart of the charge.

The "Poor" do not counter with a rejection and the development of a "freedom of the will" argument. Rather, they accept that for some of the poor, their condition is precisely the result of their nature. And even further, they concede a significant influence to other causal forces even while distinguishing the two. Ethically, this stance recognizes the place of "nurture" and "circumstances" and "environmental factors" in relation to self-determining choice. There is no polarization of "freedom" versus "determinism" in this ethical stance, Traditionally, the patristic "αὐτεξούσιον," i.e., self-determination, was always understood realistically as subject to the influence of environmental factors, while preserving the core of genuine choice.

Given this Eastern Christian ethical presupposition, it does not surprise us that the response of the "Poor" seeks to support the idea that if the "Rich" wanted to, they could choose to assume a philanthropic stance toward the "Poor." The vehicle for this argument is an appeal to an earlier period in Byzantium when Church, State, and individuals cooperated in providing a network of social care institutions, a fact extensively documented by ethicist P. Demetropoulos[37] and Byzantinist Demetrios J. Constantelos.[38] The witness of Makrembolites is more than mere nostalgia for better times, as Sevcenko seems to imply. It is an historical witness to the memory of a social concern tradition in Eastern Christianity.

> Remember ... how the men of yore, rich as you are, could not bear the pitiful sight of people worn out by various sufferings and by old age and poverty, wandering wretchedly in the midst of the city. In those days such people could either live in hostels or almshouses, or hospitals or orphanages or similar establishments. The rich of the olden days also nobly saw to the instruction of the poorest of virgins, orphans. and the needy, and to the building of

homes for young girls and the supplying of all other things of which the poor are in need. At that time the air was not filled with the groaning of any of them.[39]

The Primacy of the Ethical: Not unexpectedly and in full accordance with the line of their argument, the "Rich" do not deny the facts of the prior philanthropic concerns of their predecessors in wealth. Rather, they counter with the contention that such social concern was possible when the resources of the Empire were greater and when the order of society permitted it. But now, they say, the numbers of those having such resources are too few and the resources themselves too small to meet the need. They claim impotence in the face of such circumstances. "What can we do, few as we are, compared with the vast multitudes of the poor?"[40] they ask.

The rebuttal of the "Poor" to this argument is to concede a measure of truth to it, but to assert the primacy of the ethical imperative regardless of the circumstances and the conditions. There have always been poor, and there will always be poor, precisely because of the vagaries of circumstances such as captivity, robbery, greediness, orphanhood, shipwreck, and the calamities of life. "Want," they say in a philosophical turn of phrase, "is as necessary a part of the structure of the universe as are the elemental bodies." Together with this reality is the fact that wealth is always scarce. Precisely because the need is greater at this point in history does the moral imperative become stronger. It is the "salutary remedy which the times require."[41] Besides, even under such adverse circumstances the "Rich" receive back eternal rewards, as well as the "gratitude, prayers, praises, genuflections, eulogies, and granting you precedence; we address you almost as gods."[42]

The "Common Ownership" and Stewardship Arguments: In order to provide the warrants for the supremacy of the ethical imperative, transcending the admittedly adverse conditions of the times, Makrembolites makes use of the "common ownership" argument for social concern and philanthropy once again.

Intimately connected with the quite obsequious words quoted immediately above, is an appeal to justice based on the "common ownership" argument. It continues, "...while from you we only reclaim that which is our due."[43] As indicated earlier, there is a substratum of ethical opinion in patristic ethics of a primordial "κοινοκτημοσύνη" according to which all material good belongs to all persons equally, if only in theory. It becomes, in the Byzantine tradition, the foundation for an appeal for the stewardship of material goods by the rich for the poor, cast in a strongly religious and spiritual mode of thought. Powerfully reminiscent of Matthew 25, and loaded with its own sets of this-worldly and other-worldly moral sanctions, the passage speaks for itself, and deserves to be quoted *in toto*.

> Give us, then, what is ours, or rather give it to our common Father. For it is He who receives, even if it is we who stretch forth our hands. He is not ashamed to borrow what is His own as if it were another's and to return it again with interest. Should you show reluctance in lending to the One Who has given, He will transfer the good to other, more reasonable and trusting stewards who will not only tend to their own possessions, but also will conscientiously take care of those for whose sakes they had received them. For He is wont to introduce poverty into the affairs of the bad manager, sickness into the man who misuses health for evil ends; sometimes He makes hostility creep into harmful friendship, and servitude into a liberty pernicious to the soul. In His superior wisdom, He betters those who employ good in an evil manner, by means of an opposite action. Such has happened to many of your sort who have been rejected for lack of discretion.[44]

It would take many more pages than we have available to us to ethically "unpack" this passage. It is more than an appeal to justice, more than a reference of ethical issues to the ultimate source of the good in God, more than a concern with ethical consequences, for it is also a statement of theodicy, as well as an affirmation that human affairs are permeated with moral reality.

The "Final Defense" of Materialistic Greed: Makrembolites places in the mouths of the "Rich" a final defense of their refusal to accept their social responsibilities. Unconvinced by all that precedes, they argue that if they share the wealth none will be interested in burying them when they die, none will give them last rites and honors. The greed is presented in its naked grossness and idolatry: "Thus ... it stands to reason that we should love gold, that we should value it higher than our very souls, that acquisition and preservation should be our chief concern everywhere and that we should be ready to suffer anything for its sake."[45]

To this radical confusion of values, the "Poor" respond with a "hierarchy of values" argument. Respect and honor which is bought with gold is so low on the scale of values that it is deemed "worthless." They ask, "what is glory worth if based on considerations of business and inheritance?"[46] In contrast, "there is no higher honor for those who leave this world than a good reputation regardless of whether they are rich or poor.[47]

Theosis: Summary of Eastern Christian Ethics: The final passage under consideration serves to focus all of the argumentation of the "Poor" on the central theme of Eastern Christian ethics, *Theosis.* Here is the ultimate goal of all human ethical endeavor, God-likeness. The "Poor" pray for the "Rich" that, in spite of all, they may achieve a "splendid resurrection." "May you" they say, "be deemed worthy of it, as imitators of the merciful Christ, through His grace and love of humanity."[48] This final note goes to the core of the Eastern Christian tradition in ethics, and adequately serves to summarize its *foci* on *Theosis* and the human reflection and embodiment of divine compassion and *philanthropia.*

THE DERIVATION OF MAKREMBOLITES' ETHICS

For those familiar with contemporary ordered treatments of Eastern Orthodox ethical theory[49] it is clear that the ethical positions and stances noted in Alexios Makrembolites' "Dialogue

Between the Rich and the Poor" provides no surprises. Makrembolites is squarely in the patristic ethical tradition.

Though there are no "systematic" or "ordered" treatments of ethical theory in the patristic corpus, there is a remarkable coherence in that corpus as it deals with ethical themes. Of course, there are differing emphases and occasionally even conflicting positions on subsidiary, though significant, questions. For example, Makrembolites' strong defense of the marital state in the face of a dominant patristic interest in monasticism is not characteristic of patristic emphases. However, it does not countervail the substantive patristic teaching on marriage. It is only a different emphasis, not a disparity with patristic ethical teaching and style across the board. There is nothing new in the centrality of the *Theosis* and "Imitation of God/Christ" themes. Nor is the broad-based drawing upon varying modes of ethical argument and theories, such as natural law, divine command, consequence (utilitarian), value theory, perfectionist, prudential, and even hedonistic ethical approaches out of step with the Greek patristic ethical method. The justice arguments based on the "common ownership" theme, though far from universally espoused by the Greek Fathers, can be readily located in St. Basil and St. John Chrysostom.

Themes such as the right to property ownership; its proper use by those who temporarily hold it as stewards of God; the evil of greed, luxury and the love of money; the extremely high value placed upon philanthropy and alms-giving in Christian antiquity; and the strong theocentric and eschatological perspectives given to ethical discourse, are all characteristic of patristic ethics.

There is no doubt that the arguments are patristic, though the documentation of this conclusion would take us far beyond the confines of a paper such as this. Thus, we ask why there is no reference to patristic sources. Makrembolites only refers to the Scriptures as sources, while appealing concurrently to a natural law ethic. This, in itself, is a patristic method. But it needs to be further stated that Makrembolites would not have quoted the Fathers as authorities precisely because he stood within the living tradition of the Church's ethical teaching. He accepted them as rational, reasonable, and self-evidently valid embodiments of the Christian tradition in which he lived. Standing as he did within the ongoing, living tradition of the Church on these matters, his task was simply to present it, with the hope that his "Rich" compatriots who, though blinded by their greed, also were sharers of the tradition.

The dialogic format is not unknown in the patristic tradition. No one uses it with greater effectiveness than St. John Chrysostom, though we do not have many instances of the formal, paragraphed dialogue format. Chrysostom, however, uses the dialogic, conversational method for his exegesis and explication of biblical texts. The same pattern may be found in the canon law tradition, and in particular in Basil's *Long* and *Shorter Rules*, although there it is in the form of queries and responses.

Several passages in Makrembolites' work are decidedly Chrysostomian in style of argumentation. In particular the commingling of eternal consequences, both good and bad, with more earthbound results of moral action, and the synergistic interplay of the divine with human responsibility.

Typical is the passage above[50] in which Makrembolites argues that God could feed the poor, but He chooses to provide the resources to the wealthy in order to test their discernment and obedience, so that they may gain eternal salvation through the bestowing of mercy in this world upon the poor.

In short, it would appear accurate to hold that Makrembolites is squarely set in the patristic ethical tradition, and in particular the tradition of the great fourth century golden age of the Cappadocians and Chrysostom.

CONCLUSION

Numerous contemporary applications of this case-study are possible. I would confine myself to only two, the case study's implications for Eastern Orthodox social ethical theory and for the broader efforts by Christians to address the sphere of economic injustice in our time.

This "Dialogue" is one more piece of a long-standing, but until recently unaffirmed, tradition of social concern in Eastern Christian ethical teaching.[51] The "Dialogue" indicates that the development of a contemporary social ethic in the Orthodox Church will not have to wander far afield in finding its sources and its basic outlines. It needs to be added, for the sake of completion and balance, that the "Dialogue" is deficient in its understanding of the ethical implications of systemic evil.

Also deficient are its solutions, which are limited to the personal exercise of philanthropy. Yet once these are given, the case's perspective on social evil, the concern by those who control economic power as well as those which suffer by its abuse, is to be no less motivated by a genuine *philanthropia*. The solutions to these problems from the Church's ethical perspective of necessity will take into consideration social, political, economic, class, national, and international factors which are not prominent the "Dialogue," and, by and large, not prominent in the patristic corpus.

Nevertheless, the "Dialogue" is not completely devoid of the sociological dimensions of the issue. Its remarkable sensitivity to the class structures of Byzantine society and its sharp opposition to their worst features, while maintaining a realistic and non-ideological stance, are refreshingly candid openings toward a more modern perspective.

At the same time, the "Dialogue" employs the same perspectives and understandings that many contemporary ethical systems affirm. However, the dependency of much contemporary Christian social justice concern upon Marxist categories is shown to be far from necessary. There are resources within the tradition of the Church that, if properly developed and exploited, could address questions of systemic economic injustice without recourse to a world-view which is at heart inimical to the Christian faith.

ENDNOTES

* Presented at the Annual Meeting of the Society of Christian Ethics in January of 1984, the 25th anniversary of the Society. The study was published in *The Annual of the Society of Christian Ethics – 1984,* Vancouver, B.C.: Society of Christian Ethics, 1984, pp. 315-340.

[1] Ihor Sevcenko, *Society and Intellectual Life in Late Byzantium.* London: Variorum Reprints, 1981, Ch. VII, "Alexios Makrembolites and his 'Dialogue Between the Rich and the Poor,'" pp. 188-228.

[2] A.A. Vasiliev, *History of the Byzantine Empire.* Madison: University of Wisconsin Press, 1971, vol. II, p. 683.

[3] Ibid.

[4] Tafrali, *Thessalonique des origines au XIV siecle.* Paris, 1919, p. 224.

[5] Quoted in P. Charanis, "Internal Strife in Byzantium," *Byzantion,* xv, p. 217.

[6] *Sabbaiticus* 417.

[7] A. Papadopoulos-Kerameus, *Hierosolymitike Bibliotheke*, II, Petrograd, 1894, Vol. II. pp. 555-556. See also the new edition of this work, Bruxelles: *Culture et Civilisation,* 1963, Vol. II, pp. 534-536.

[8] I am here following Papadopoulos-Kerameus, and supplementing my comments primarily from Sevcenko's description of the manuscript in Note 12, page 189 of the introductory comments.

[9] By Papadopoulos-Kerameus.

[10] See Sevcenko's footnote 11, p. 189 and Papadopoulos-Kerameus' footnote 1 on p. 536 of the Brussels edition.

[11] See Sevcenko's extensive and insightful analysis of the class dynamics evident in the "Dialogue" on pp. 200-202.

[12] There are eleven distinct exchanges between the two parties of the "Dialogue," a defense or charge by the "Rich" with a response by the "Poor." In the description that follows, however, I have grouped some of these when they deal with essentially the same topic.

[13] Reference will be made to the English translation by Sevcenko as "Text" and the page numbers in his study mentioned above. Text, p. 216.

[14] Text, p. 217.

[15] Text, p. 216.

[16] Text, p. 218.

[17]Text, p. 217.

[18]Text, p. 218.

[19]Text, p. 219.

[20]Text, p. 219.

[21]Text, p. 219.

[22]Text, p. 220.

[23]Text, p. 220.

[24]Text, p. 220.

[25]Text, p. 220.

[26]Text, p. 221.

[27]Text, p. 222.

[28]Text, p. 222. Included in this exchange is a remarkably frank and concrete description of the contrasts between the lifestyles of the two classes. It serves to convince the reader of the dialogue that it is much more than an intellectual exercise.

[29]Text, pp. 222-223.

[30]Text, p. 223.

[31]Text, p. 223.

[32]Text, p. 223.

[33]Text, p. 224.

[34]Text, p. 224.

[35]Text, p. 224.

[36]Text, p. 224.

[37] Ἡ Πίστις τῆς Ἀρχαίας Ἐκκλησίας Ὡς Κανών τῆς Ζωῆς καί ὁ Κόσμος (*The Faith of the Ancient Church as a Rule of Life and the World*), Athens, 1959, which treats the subject to the sixth century.

[38]See *Byzantine Philanthropy and Social Welfare.* New Brunswick, N.J.: Rutgers University Press, 1968, for the sixth to the eleventh centuries. Constantelos has in press a book which carries the investigation on to the end of the Byzantine Empire in 1453.(N.b., Published subsequently under the title *Poverty, Society and Philanthropy in the Late Mediaeval Greek World.* New Rochelle, NY: A. D. Caratzas, 1992.)

[39]Text, p. 225.

[40]Text, p. 225.

[41]Text, p. 226.

[42]Text, p. 226.

[43]Text, p. 226.

[44]Text, pp. 226-227.
[45]Text, p. 227.
[46]Text, p. 227.
[47]Text, pp. 227-228.
[48]Text, p. 228.
[49]See Stanley S. Harakas, *Toward Transfigured Life: The* Theoria *of Eastern Orthodox Ethics.* Light and Life Publishing Co., 1983. For a summary statement of Eastern Orthodox Ethics, see pp. 26-38.
[50]Text, p. 224.
[51]Stanley S. Harakas, *Let Mercy Abound: Social Concern in the Greek Orthodox Church.* Brookline, MA: Holy Cross Orthodox Press, 1983. Chapter 1 includes an extensive bibliography.

10

RESPONDING TO CONTEMPORARY CHALLENGES TO ORTHODOXY[*]

In September of 1993, I participated in a Conference on "Crisis of Cultures and the Birth of Faith" at Loyola Marymount University in Los Angeles. One section of the conference was labeled "Church vs. State or Religious Freedom vs. Intolerance."

This context troubled me as an Eastern Orthodox theologian because of the way the issue was framed. In a thoroughly Western fashion it assumed a conflicting and adversarial relationship of Church and State (i.e., "Church vs. State") and counters "Religious Freedom" with "Intolerance." One of the assumptions of this formulation is that no other arrangement in the relationships between Church and state is possible. Further, it implies that the primary relationship between Church and "that which is not Church" is the relationship of the Church to the state. Another assumption, it would appear, is that the American constitutional understanding of religious freedom, or even that freedom itself, is primarily a political category, that has as its antipode, the negative stance of intolerance.

This description is a summary of both the challenges and the opportunities that the contemporary world offers to Eastern Orthodox Christianity. It seems, further, that the contemporary dominant pluralist, rationalist, capitalist, secular, materialist, existentialist, and individualist milieu of the modern world challenges not only Eastern Christianity, not only the Roman Catholic and Protestant embodiments of Western Christianity, but also every religious tradition rooted in the conviction of the existence and importance for human life of a reality that is transcendent to the empirically experienced world.

Nevertheless, is accurate to say that Eastern Christianity is challenged in unique ways by the modern world. This is true, particularly, after the dissolution of the tensions between the socialist/communist regimes of Eastern Europe and the Western world, and the default entry of the nations of that region into the family of nations of the western capitalist-based democracies.

I seek in this paper to address this situation as it impacts on the Orthodox Church in the form of challenges to its traditional ethos and *modus operandi.* Not all of these challenges are external, however. The position that I will espouse in this paper is that the primary challenges to contemporary, empirical Orthodox Christianity are the consequences of a failure of Eastern Orthodoxy today to fully comprehend its own faith tradition. If it did, it would, rather, be in the position of challenging, rather than to being challenged by contemporary world dynamics.

Consequently, the first part of this paper seeks to address a fundamental question for the Orthodox Church that raises the issue of the relationship of the Church to the "world," or perhaps more neutrally phrased, the relationship of the Church to that which is more or less "not Church." A major portion of this paper will be an effort to show that for a number of reasons, the contemporary Orthodox Church suffers from a failure to practically grasp its own biblico-patristic tradition as it seeks to live out its mandate as Church in the world, i.e., in the midst of that which is not Church.

I intend to follow this more or less theological assessment with a few specific topics that are, in my judgment, particularly challenging and concurrently illuminating for this inquiry and ultimately, for the Eastern Orthodox Church in its own present journey. But the major focus will be on the question of Orthodox Christianity and contemporary aspects of ethnic and national identity coupled with the issue of religious freedom.

The paper will conclude with some normative criteria and suggested guidelines for the Eastern Orthodox Church in the post-Soviet world as it seeks to remain faithful both to its tradition and its call to fulfill the mission to which its Lord has called it.

WEST AND EAST MEET: THEY DO NOT UNDERSTAND EACH OTHER

I will begin this section with a description of an exchange that took place in the Geneva suburb of Chambesy in September of 1991 at the Inter-Orthodox Center of the Ecumenical Patriarchate. It was a meeting of representatives of the Autocephalous Orthodox Churches throughout the world, and, of course, dominated by representatives of Orthodox Churches from Eastern Europe.

The meeting was chaired by then Metropolitan and now Ecumenical Patriarch Bartholomew. The topic of discussion was a decision expressed in the report of the Orthodox representation at the Seventh General Assembly of the World Council of Churches in Canberra the previous February. In that report the Orthodox expressed serious dissatisfactions with tendencies in the WCC that seemed to them to be moving the body away from its fundamental mission of fostering church unity among Christians. Having raised the issue of whether the Orthodox Churches should continue their membership in the WCC in that statement, representatives of the Orthodox Churches met in Chambesy seven months later to address it.[1]

Patriarch Bartholomew began the meeting by inviting each of the hierarchs of the various Autocephalous Churches to describe the situation in the local Church which they represented. Almost all of the church leaders who spoke expressed themselves, roughly, in the following fashion:

> We are very pleased that our Church is now free from control and repression at the hands of the former regime. We rejoice in our newfound freedom. We look forward to a normalization of our Church life. Yet, we are disturbed

> by the inrush of foreign missionaries, from various Chris-
> tian and non-Christian churches and sects. They are cre-
> ating division and fragmenting our national and ecclesial
> unity in a scandalous way.
> We ask you to protest this inappropriate activity, for our
> nation is an Orthodox nation by tradition and polity. Other
> Churches should respect that and stop seeking to convert
> our people.

This was the almost unanimous stance from the leaders of
the Orthodox Churches present at the meeting. In my role as a
"theological consultant," I felt it necessary to speak to this stance.
I began by noting that I was speaking as an Orthodox who shares
in a traditional ethnic heritage but also as an American. I repeatedly sought to point out that there seemed to be an inherent contradiction in the statements celebrating freedom on the
one hand and, on the other, demanding that non-Orthodox
proselytizing activity be prohibited. I offered the opinion that
from a contemporary, western, capitalist point of view these
were mutually exclusive concepts. What was needed, I said, was
an acceptance of the new realities based not any more on social-
ism, but on capitalist realities, rooted in a competitive effort to
retain and regain for the Orthodox Church the péoples who
were its traditional flock. Essentially, I called for a pastoral ac-
tivism. This meant that it was necessary for the Orthodox
Churches of Eastern Europe and elsewhere, to accept that in
the new world of capitalist domination, freedom meant that
anyone could proclaim their beliefs and seek converts, but that
the best defense by the Orthodox Church would be to minister
energetically to their natural constituencies.

I was repeatedly told that "I did not understand," and my
comments essentially fell on deaf, if not antagonistic ears. This
personal experience summarizes the general problem of the challenge of the post-Soviet world on the Orthodox. The Orthodox
assumptions for ecclesial life are not rooted in the western post-
enlightenment, secularist, capitalist, and individualistic ethos
now so dominant in the modern world. The theological, cul-

tural and social mind-set of Eastern Orthodoxy, rather, calls for a stance that emphasizes a radically different worldview.

In the face of western rationalism, the Orthodox constantly emphasize the transcendent mystery of the ultimate unknowability of God and the finiteness of human conceptualization before truth. While the elusive dream of Kant's Pure Reason continues to underlie western technological progress, the East's stance is summarized in the title given to a recent translation and commentary of Gregory the Theologian's five theological orations by Fredrick W. Norris: *Faith Gives Fullness to Reasoning.*[2] Recent epistemological discussions in postmodernist philosophical theology, however, may be moving toward the traditional Eastern approaches to theological knowledge that posits kataphatic (propositional, positive, foundational) knowledge within a larger context of apophatic understandings of knowledge (the *via negativa*). Such views seek a more aesthetic, or intuitive, or a more "practical reason" (i.e., Aristotelian Φρόνησις) approach to knowledge.[3] But the gulf certainly has not yet been bridged between East and West, as yet on the question of how truth is apprehended.

Contrary to the secularism dominant in the modern world, Eastern Orthodoxy has a sacramental perspective that looks for the transfiguration of life through its liturgical and spiritual incorporation into the life of the Kingdom, while affirming its created reality. As liturgiologist Alkiviadis Calivas has put it, "God's life is infused into the present age and mingled with it, without change or confusion, through the mysteries (sacraments). God touches, purifies, illumines, sanctifies and deifies human life in his uncreated divine energies through the mysteries."[4] Or, conversely, as liturgiologist Alexander Schmemann preferred to describe the sacramental life, the ordinary activities of human life are incorporated into the life of the Kingdom.[5] Both models are to be found in the theological and spiritual literature of Eastern Orthodoxy. Either and both are in radical contradiction with the dominant western secular perspectives of the essential unimportance of the divine for modern life.

In sharp distinction from the rampant individualism of the contemporary mind set, in Orthodoxy, both theological and ethnic considerations play important roles in affirming, rather, the corporate reality of human existence and peoplehood. For example, in his presentation "Holy Spirit, Renew and Sanctify Our Life" at the 7th Assembly of the World Council of Churches, Metropolitan John of Pergamon (Zizioulas) argued that in the face of the fact that holiness is often thought of in individual terms, it is often forgotten that the presence of the Holy Spirit creates community. In Zizioulas' Orthodox perspective, "Individualistic holiness is something that cannot exist."[6]

An outgrowth of this perspective is the incarnational missionary perspective of Orthodox Christianity that historically sought to embody the Christian faith in the language, culture, ethos, and lifestyle of particular peoples and nations. This formation of "nations" (as distinguished from states), in a way that respected the local identities and cultures of believers was characteristic of Byzantine missions from the earliest history of Eastern Christianity. One could argue that the writing of the New Testament in the "Κοινή" Greek language – the dominant common spoken language of the first century Roman Empire – was a precursor of this practice.

James Stamoolis, an Evangelical Protestant scholar, in his work *Eastern Orthodox Mission Theology Today* emphasizes the importance of this approach for Orthodox Christianity. He says, "The incarnational approach, the translation into the vernacular yet more than the translation, the very embodiment of God's truth in the language and culture of a people, has been the hallmark of the best of Orthodox mission work."[7]

It is a commonplace in the sociology of religion to point to the unique confluence of Protestantism, the Enlightenment, the breakdown of Feudalism, and the appearance of the nation-state as important sources for the development of capitalism and the secularist mentality.[8]

In the earlier Christian period efforts were made to subject economic activity to the spiritual and sacramental Christian perspective, though there were without question, "contradictions and accommodations" in L. William Countryman's phrase.[9]

A permanent part of that legacy is the unwillingness to accept as adequate to the human situation of the economic interpretation of the human condition. In his book *Social Thought* in the series "The Message of the Fathers of the Church," Peter Phan has provided students with a useful collection of patristic texts that express the view that the economic dimension of life is also subject to the transfiguring presence of God, as well as its incorporation in the life of the Kingdom of God.[10]

On other points, as well, the social teaching of the Fathers should continue to shape the social teaching of the Church today. Among these are the affirmation of the basic equality of all human beings; the doctrine of the right of private ownership; the principle that the material goods are destined by God for the use of all human beings to satisfy their basic needs; the insistence on the necessity of conversion of heart and detachment from earthly possessions; the inculcation of the duty of almsgiving not only out of charity but also of justice; the doctrine of the identity of Christ with the poor. These elements are the perennial heritage that the Church should cherish and preserve in presenting its message of solidarity and hope to the world of today.[11]

Soviet communism, and Marxism in general, presented an economic materialist interpretation of human existence. In the end, this vision failed; but long before the tree collapsed, the people of the communist block had perceived that the heart of the trunk had rotted away. Such a sterile vision of human life could feed the soul of neither individuals nor societies. The modern world now functions primarily with a self-policing capitalist economy. There are serious structural dangers within it, also. The Orthodox Church and the world at large will no doubt have to live with it for a long time. But the Church's patristic heritage cannot allow it or the world to become comfortable with it, for in many ways it is not less materialist and unconformable with wholesome social living than its erstwhile economic competitor.

A final outgrowth of the modern mind-set that stands at odds with the received ethos of Eastern Orthodox Christianity is the acceptance of culture and value of pluralism as it applies to how a society or nation identifies itself. Americans tend to think of the principles of the Constitution of the United States as a blueprint for all human societies. Mediated by a significant intellectual respect for human rights, these views have in many ways created a kind of cultural imperialism that fosters the break-up of long-standing cultures, nations, and societies by minimizing the significance of shared corporate identities.

Yet, there is a modern litany of failures in United States public policies where regard for cultural and ethnic corporate identities has been too minimal, on the assumption that principles of American pluralism and individualism are self-evidently superior: the divided nations of Korea, Vietnam, Palestine and the State of Israel, the former Yugoslavia, Haiti, Somalia and Rwanda are a few examples.

The ethnically coherent societies of Europe are also aware of these tensions. Witness the problems of Germany with the communities of immigrant workers; the French with the Algerian minority, the claims to ethnic self-determination by Czechs, Slovaks, Serbs, Slovenes, Croats, Albanians, Basques, and Irish.

Few societies are presently able to tolerate the pluralism of the United States. The tears in the social fabric of the United States along racial, ethnic, economic, religious, and cultural lines do not auger well for its own future, as it seeks concurrently to export pluralism to other nations and traditions without resolving its own inner tensions.

The useful studies of Robert Bellah, *Habits of the Heart* and *The Good Society*, point beyond individual interests to the commonly shared life of a people in its corporate life and shared institutions.[12]

These studies point to broader symptoms. While the topic of this paper is the challenges of the modern age to the Orthodox, this issue is not limited to the Orthodox. Both religious and non-religious communities are now at risk. The Lockean construct of society as a collection of autonomous individuals is not only a threat to the corporate understanding of the Church. Pushed too strongly, in the form of radical pluralism as is fostered in the modern world, it is a challenge to the modern world itself.

THE THEOLOGICAL CHALLENGE

These and similar conflicts between the Eastern Christian ethos and the modern post-Soviet world create a whole range of challenges for Eastern Orthodoxy as we move toward the beginning of the Third Millennium. It is my contention, however, that these large-scale cultural challenges are being poorly met by the Orthodox Church. This is so because of the inability of the Orthodox Church to comprehend the fullness of its own theology, especially its own theology regarding its relationships on the personal plane, the ecclesial dimension, and in its outreach mission.

In a telling passage, historian and theologian Demetrios Constantelos provides one example in modern Orthodox thought regarding this issue. He holds that the contemporary exclusive focus on the Eucharist is a case in point. The light of Orthodox theology is limited so sharply to this one aspect of its life that it effectively rules out consideration of other important and greatly needed aspects for a full and adequate understanding of the Orthodox Christian faith. Discussing Orthodox ethics and social concern, Constantelos writes:

> ... Orthodox theologians today tend to consider liturgical theology and eucharistic ecclesiology as being the most important aspects of Orthodox theology, (yet) there are many others ... who maintain that Orthodoxy's social character has not received the theological attention it deserves.[13]

In particular this has often meant a reductionism among the Orthodox in the understanding of the Faith. Often this has expressed itself in rubrics such as "Orthodoxy is the Eucharist," or "Orthodoxy is the Jesus Prayer," or "Orthodoxy is nothing but love," or "Orthodoxy is Mystical Communion," or "Orthodoxy is the life of Repentance," or "True Orthodoxy is Monasticism" or "Orthodoxy is fully embodied in the Icon," or "Orthodoxy is the Patristic Mind," etc.

In my own studies, I have resisted such reductionisms. In several articles I have sought to develop an understanding of Orthodox Christianity that is based on the creative, redemptive and sanctifying energies of the persons of the Holy Trinity as they are expressed in three interpenetrating spheres of existence: the personal experience of God, the corporate life of the Church, and the outreach in mission, philanthropy and social concern to the world, that is, that which is not Church.[14]

The danger, of course, is to reduce the theological under-standing of Orthodox Christianity either to the personal sphere, or to ecclesial life narrowly (eucharistically) understood, or to the outreach dimensions of the faith. Once any of these be-comes so dominant that it minimizes the others, then the abil-ity of Orthodox thought and life to adequately address the chal-lenges of any age and time is severely crippled.

Such a reductionism has also taken place among Orthodox theologians as they assess the relationship of the Church to the world. Because this has direct impact on the topic of this paper, I believe it would be useful to describe these variant approaches. They may even serve to illuminate the reactions of the repre-sentatives at the Chambesy meeting described at the beginning of this paper.[15]

As a heuristic exercise, I wish to present three contemporary Orthodox writers on the subject of faith and culture whose views are significantly diverse and who illustrate the range of current opinion in the Orthodox Church on the subject. To these con-temporary viewpoints, I wish to present also my own perspective as a constructive alternative to the apparent mutual exclusivity of these contemporary views.

The three authors whom I will present and discuss are Michael Azkoul with his "Other Worldly" approach to the issue of the relationship of culture and faith, Vigen Guroian, with his "Detached/Critical" approach, and Metropolitan George Khodre's "Universalist" approach. My own view on the subject could be labeled an "Integrative/Wholistic" way of accessing the issue.

A very powerful statement expressing an antagonistic relationship between the Orthodox Church and the culture of that which is not Church is to be found in an article titled "The Greek Fathers: Polis and Paideia" by Fr. Michael Azkoul.[16]

Arising precisely out of the antagonistic ecclesial/state relationships of post-revolutionary Soviet life, Azkoul represents those who responded to the negation of spiritual values in both East and West, by building high walls of separation and discontinuity between worldly culture and the Church.

This was not the only course of action open to the Orthodox. Others, for example, also addressed the post-Second World War society of Europe with concepts focusing on the negation of spiritual values, but saw that period as an opportunity for mission to and responsibility for the world, as represented by Greek author Alexander Tsirindanes.[17]

Azkoul's perspective is much more negative. He focuses on what he perceives to be an essential contradiction between the "City of God," and the "City of Man," presented as two cities in essential and substantive conflict. This thesis is stated by Azkoul clearly in the following passage.

> The concern of the Greek Fathers was precisely the classical *polis* and its challenge to the Christian Economy. We will see that they rejected the Greek *paideia* only *qua* the servant of the *polis* with its moral, religious ideals and its ontological implications. If, too, the Fathers reserved special venom for Greek philosophy, "the foreign philosophy," it was because it was for the Greeks the ultimate weapon in the defense of the classical world-view at whose heart stood the *polis*. Of course, at stake in the conflict was salvation in Christ, a salvation which the Fathers declared could not be found apart from the Church, their *polis* and *paideia*.[18]

The linguistic character of this passage is important. The words used denote clash, rivalry, and combat. For Azkoul, Greek philosophy is the enemy's "ultimate weapon," used in a "battle" and "conflict" between Christianity and pagan culture. The two πόλεις and παιδεῖαι are sharply distinct and their relationship is one of rivalry, strife, and struggle. They are at war.

What Azkoul sees in the pagan Greco-Roman *polis* with its institutions supported by pagan religion is fundamentally opposed and antagonistic to the world-view of the Christian polis.

Consequently, the παιδεία of the Greek city-state was inseparable from the pagan religious worldview. The laws of the polis regulated the relationships of citizen-individuals. The mission of the Greek polis was to spread the explicitly classic pagan worldview among other peoples and cultures through her "arts, thought, and political order."[19]

Similarly, Azkoul sees the Church Fathers as understanding the New Testament and the Church as being in radical contrast with the Greek world-view. The Church is "another city," a Kingdom not of the world but of God. Salvation is precisely "from the world." The Church is the "new order," and the "true kingdom," opposed to the "principalities and powers" of the Greek πόλις. It is experienced liturgically as the "eighth day," and intellectually as the "new σοφία" and a totally new way of life, a new φιλοσοφία in clear and sharp discontinuity with the old which is lived out in the old βίος φιλοσοφικὸς of the pagans.

His reading of the Church Fathers focuses on passages that emphasize the discontinuities between Church and world. For example, he acknowledges Basil's respect for potential good elements in the non-Christian culture of his times, but he emphasizes his statements which contrast Greek παιδεία with Christianity in an "either/or" fashion, admitting only to an occasional use of the pagan tradition by Basil. In Azkoul's reading, Church and world are "two different cities, based on different faiths, similar methods, and irreconcilable aims (that) produced opposite kinds of men."[20]

Translated into the present, this view allows for a minimal, otherwise unavoidable contact with the world which is not Church, but which is dominated by a polemical, antithetical and antagonistic attitude toward it. Only a Christian culture is acceptable for the Christian. Between Christian culture and that which is not specifically Christian culture there is only opposition. Those who are familiar with Ernst Troeltsch's "Sect Type," will find in Azkoul a ready example.[21]

Somewhat different, though related, is the position espoused by Vigen Guroian, an Armenian Orthodox theologian, teaching, living, and writing in the United States. I call his view a "Detached/Critical" approach. His major work illustrating this view is a collection of essays on various topics of Orthodox ethics published under the title *Incarnate Love: Essays in Orthodox Ethics.*[22] However, in subsequent publications this stance has been modified significantly. Guroian's thought on issues of social ethics is molded into an almost exclusively sacramental and eschatological framework, functioning best as a method of heuristic critique and vision-building rather than as a method for providing concrete guidance to the faithful for living. Cast primarily in terms of a virtue ethic, Guroian's approach has the strength of providing a critique of existing practice both within and outside the Church. From his viewpoint, Orthodox ethics is discontinuous with culture, but not totally so. The major role of Orthodox ethics is discovered in the contrast between the Christian vision of life, marked by virtues peculiar to the Christian way of life, and the fallen existence of the world.

Unlike Azkoul, however, the major motif that governs the relationship of Christian faith to culture and society is not antagonism and war, but critique and witness. There is a concern, a concern for the world and its well-being that is expressed by calling it to repentance and to faith.

In the specifically "Social Ethics" part of the volume, the author presents what he feels is a radical departure from past approaches of Faith and Culture in the Orthodox world. This past he understands to be a compromised excessive "Constantinian" stance of Orthodox Christianity in its relationship to culture, society and the state. It is here that Guroian functions best as an exponent of a relatively widespread view in Orthodox ethics today, which does its work with an almost exclusive liturgical or eucharistic emphasis. In Guroian's perspective, this emphasis in practice requires the Orthodox to relate to cultures not their own in the world about them precisely as Orthodox Christians in a prophetic or critical role, but which would also appear to essentially disengage them from the societies in which they live.[23]

Guroian's social ethic is dependent on Orthodox views steeped in eucharistic theological concepts, as well as on some contemporary Protestant writers who are rejecting the liberal social ethics of a previous generation. The focus on eucharistic ecclesiology as the "all in all" of Orthodox life, easily transforms itself in the last analysis to a separatist mentality. In addition there is a strong influence in Guroian's writing of Protestant theologians Stanley Hauerwas and John Howard Yoder. Their views approach culture and society essentially in a mode of critique, together with the presentation of the example of the Christian way, but without much expectation that this stance can influence much of the life of that which is not Church.

The end result of Guroian's work is to lift up the discontinuous aspect of the Church's identity in relationship to that which is not of the Kingdom to a more prominent place in contemporary Orthodox thinking. There seems to be an almost exclusive focus and advocacy of the need for the Church to maintain a critical stance of culture and society, a posture which he describes as the "prophetic" role of the Church *vis a vis* the culture and society in which the Orthodox find themselves.

This perspective is readily applicable to the recent past of the Soviet era. It provokes some significant suggestions for the correction of caesropapist tendencies in Orthodox practice, and in particular its alleged subservience to political authority and capitulation to and compromise not only with the Soviet system, but with cultures and ethnic identities, as well.

Guroian's critique is well posited. All Orthodox must admit that by and large, the prophetic role is not one which the Orthodox have cultivated as of late. This is especially true during and following the period enslavement in the Ottoman Empire (15-19th centuries), and the period of ecclesial decapitation of the Church in Russia from time of Tsar Peter the Great to the Bolshevik takeover of the Russian Revolution. Guroian and others, such as Alexander Webster, make a needed and in many ways valid critique.[24]

As a result of his analysis, Guroian accuses most of contemporary Orthodoxy and others of having adopted a "neo-Constantinianism," which amounts to "the surrender of their evangelical witness (which is)... compounded by a long history of compromise and accommodation..."[25] In contrast, he proposes a missionary stance that is proclamatory of both the condemnation of sin and the good news of the Gospel, while presenting an example for the modeling of society. The distinct impression is that the proclaiming and model-giving keeps the proclaimer and model essentially distant from, and otherwise unrelated to the object of these efforts.

One need not reject the prophetic stance, or criticism of self or others, to note that the issue is whether the prophetic stance is the only message and the only focus that ought to characterize the relationship of Orthodox Christianity to culture outside its own boundaries.

Guroian's view emphasizes the discontinuities between the Church and culture, to the point that its major alternative is prophetic criticism. Its strength is that it does not allow for complacency with past solutions. But its weakness is that it is admittedly not only discontinuous with present society, but it is also discontinuous with the Orthodox Church's own centuries long tradition. There seems to be little if any place for an appreciation of culture for its own sake, much less an acceptance of the task of transforming culture – as much as it is capable of transformation. Nor is there any sense of responsibility for addressing and correcting injustices in the "fallen world." As articulated, this perspective, intentionally or unintentionally, fosters an uninvolved stance toward society and culture. It is not so strongly expressed as is the confrontationalist stance of Michael Azkoul, but it is, in effect, almost the same with the exception that contact with culture is motivated not by opposition and enmity, but by an evangelical proclamation which calls for repentance on the part of culture and the presentation to culture of an alternative way of living in a paradigmatic style, trusting in its power to transform.

In sharp contrast with the preceding two approaches are the views of Metropolitan George Khodre which I call a "Universalist" position that is inclusive and world-affirming. In contrast to the theologians discussed previously, his is an affirmation of a mutual relationship between worldly culture and faith, and ethically speaking, a call to transfigure culture, as well as to learn from it.

His ideas were developed in an article published under the title "The Church and the World."[26] Khodre's thesis is that on the one hand, the world is a part of the Church, and on the other, that the Church is part of the world. The two entities are not mutually exclusive, nor are they fundamentally opposed to each other. Khodre strongly and powerfully rejects dualistic approaches which "excessive monasticism" has produced. He rejects these as not genuine expressions of the Orthodox Christian faith and expresses the need to articulate and live out this experience in the light of what he calls "the happy failure of historical Christendom."

For him, the Church and the world share a common existence. He bases his view on the creation belief that the world in which the Church finds itself has been created good by God and in the soteriological faith that the Church is the divinely established means for the world's salvation.

The consequence of these affirmations is the truth of divine Love, in which both the Church and the world are objects of God's love. They are essentially the same in the purview of divine love. This unified perspective determines that the mission of the Church is precisely "for the world." But Khodre goes much further than Guroian does in defining this mission. For

Khodre, the Church is the heart of a renewed humanity. Consequently, its *raison d'être* is precisely to be "in the world" and "for the world." Correctly understood, Khodre avers, the Church has the role of discerning the "signs of the times" for the world, revealing to it as well, the God who is present, yet hidden in its midst. The eschatological vision of the Church is not foreign to the world, which in the strict sense is not "the Church." It includes the world and its culture in that vision, and affirms it as the object of God's redemptive work.

This has significant consequences for Khodre. First, both the Church and the world share in evil. It is wrong for the Church to compare its "eschatological purity" with the sinfulness of the world. Both Church and world move together toward renewal. God works in both, fulfilling His will. Consequently the Christian cannot be divorced from life in the world. The Christian disciple must live a life which is in communion with God through and in the Church, but the disciple cannot realize that communion with God, without being in communion with his or her own generation, and with its life, problems, and culture. In truth, however, the Christian will focus on the spiritual side of the dimensions of culture. For example, the task of the Christian is not only to label and name the evils of technology, but also to lift up the spirit and human goals of technology, its sacramental purpose and use.

Khodre is painfully aware of the failures of historic Orthodoxy to address its responsibilities to the world especially in those cases when the Orthodox have historically been subservient to their cultures. He says: "It is heart-rending to realize that historical Orthodoxy is incapable of witnessing publicly in front of the established structures and that it so comfortably joins a pseudo-monastic manichaism to an enslaved bourgeois conservatism." Khodre sees this as producing a "kind of ecclesial monism" among many Orthodox, "which is historically destroying the Church-world relation."

He would rather that the Church become fully aware and sensitive to its intimate relationship with the world. And giving a wholly different context to the prophetic role of the Church, he writes:

> The Church is made eschatologically present before God, not before the world... (As such) it is that to which humanity aspires, the icon of that which humanity is called to become, and by this very fact, like the icon, it is made of this same stock of humanity through a light that comes from above. It is, to the profit of this same humanity, a promise of transfiguration. Because of this vocation, the Church is the heart of this humanity ... The prophetic function with which the Church is entrusted among other functions actually consists in revealing to the world the God hidden in its midst as a means of causing history to conform to its own end, which is the manifestation of the new Jerusalem. But it is actually the world which constitutes the framework for prophesy as it constitutes the field in which the witness of holiness shines in silence.[27]

The tonality of this passage is neither one of antagonism, nor of a discontinuity so sharp that it allows only for a distant proclamation or a detached exemplarism of the Church toward the world. Thus, he says, "If we can establish the fact that there are no two spheres of spiritual existence from the theological as well as the ethical point of view, we can point to the fact that the activity of Christians goes on at the same time both within the sanctuary and without it."[28]

Given this viewpoint, there is no fundamental antinomy between faith and culture, but only a right or wrong relationship between faith and culture, relationships that cannot be only one of words, but of action as well. A right relationship between faith and the world's culture lives in "the hope that the Christian world will set out towards an actually lived social reality."[29] In such a perspective, culture becomes the material substance into which faith is incarnated. Khodre's perspective is universal, inclusive, involved, and activist.

My own view seeks to hold the values of these three approaches together. I call it an "Integrative-Wholistic" approach to culture that seeks to affirm the positive and constructive aspects of these and similar approaches. It acknowledges the tensions that their claims make on believers individually and the Church as a whole, and seeks to avoid the temptation to reductionism that will make the relationship of the Church with the world's culture into a formula or ideology.

When Christian theologians seek to understand and articulate the relationship between faith and culture a primary, overarching, and governing condition of such reflection is the fundamental Christian truth that God "has put all things under (Jesus') feet and has made him the head over all things for the church," making Jesus Christ "the fullness of him who fills all in all."[30] This primacy, and inclusiveness of Christ over all things, including human culture, is the key for a Christian approach to the relationship of faith to culture.

In the three representative writings described above, this fundamental truth is either consciously or unconsciously posited. Yet, they have come to significantly different prescriptions for the Church's relationship to the world. In my view, the appropriate course of action is not to seek to choose which one of these views is the exclusively correct one, to the exclusion of the others. Rather, it is necessary to affirm precisely how in each, there is an expression of "the fullness of him who fills all in all."

This needs to take place while limiting conclusions drawn from each of them that would tend to absolutize their impact upon the relationship of faith and culture. I am convinced that the Orthodox experience of the relationship of the Faith to culture, and of the Church to the world, cannot choose among these apparently conflicting views. Each of these affirms at least one major aspect of the Christian faith and the Church, as they relate to culture and the world.

There are scriptural, patristic, canonical, liturgical, sacramental, and doctrinal supports for each – and all – of these three stances. There is an "ethical trinity" that must be grasped and held in the wholeness of faith and life.

Thus, there is an integrity and strength in the affirmation

that the Church is in fact "a new city" whose essence is not that of the "old city." It is necessary to affirm and recognize that there is a "mind of the world and its culture" which is under satanic dominion, which is actively at war with all that is sub-sumed under "the mind of Christ" and stands in opposition to it. Azkoul's focus is a continual reminder that there is a per-petual battle against these principalities and powers of the present age. There is a genuine danger that Christians will become too accommodated to the world. Azkoul's response to the question of faith and culture provokes the Church and its members to remember its call to purity, faithfulness, commitment, sanctity, and growth in the image of God and the Kingdom. But there is more to the relationship of faith and culture, and as a result, an exclusive call to battle the forces of the earthly city is too limited a vocation for those who would relate faith and culture.[31]

Guroian's analysis calls Orthodox Christians to re-examine their historically all-too-compliant relationship with cultural and political authority. He is saying that in the contemporary plu-ralistic setting of twentieth-century America, we have an op-portunity to shake free the shackles of cultural subservience so as "to proclaim the message fully, that all the Gentiles might hear it."[32]

He is saying that the Orthodox cannot do that with credibil-ity if they are not self-critical, and ready to name in a prophetic way the falsehoods of our age, which the Orthodox themselves often embody. But even more importantly, he reminds the Or-thodox of what they are called to be in practice and in life, i.e., an embodiment of what they profess. It requires a stance that in prophetic fashion names evil wherever it expresses itself, as well a "virtue ethic." But that alone is not adequate to the prompt-ing of Orthodox theological awareness in the sphere of the en-counter with culture in the societies in which we live.

But further, the vision of the Kingdom must also be incar-nated in the societies and cultures in which we live in order to move them, change them, ultimately convert, and transform them – as much as they are capable of it – into vehicles of Kingdom living. That is the message of Metropolitan George Khodre, in the final analysis. He reminds us of the need to reach out, to infuse cultures with God's goodness. Khodre affirms a relation to culture by Christians and the Church in the spirit of the passage in Philippians which affirms and encourages "whatever is true, whatever honorable, whatever is just, whatever is pure, whatever lovely, whatever is gracious, if there is any excellence, if there is anything worthy of praise."[33]

A stance that is able to condemn what is evil and to separate from it, to courageously and prophetically speak to a fallen and distorted world seeking its correction, repentance, and reform, but also to affirm its most wholesome values, seems to reflect a good portion of the patristic tradition of Eastern Orthodoxy, while standing in solidarity with those who suffer the consequences of the evil in the world. Such a wholistic and integrated approach can serve the Orthodox Church well as it seeks to face the challenges it encounters in a rapidly developing and changing social and cultural situations.

It is to some of these particular issues that we now turn, keeping in mind the first part of this paper that sought to document a substantial difference in thought between Eastern Christian and Western values and assumptions on the one hand, and the need for the Orthodox to avoid simplistic formula-like approaches to their understandings of the relationship of the Church and the cultures of the world.

THE RANGE OF CHALLENGES TO ORTHODOXY IN THE MODERN WORLD

In many ways, Eastern Orthodox Christianity is no different than Roman Catholicism and the various strains of Protestantism as they face the modern world. The secular character of the modern world's ethos and values in many ways militates against the values of faith. It is also true that in many ways, the world's values frequently serve to set the agenda for the Church as it seeks to engage with that which is not Church. For example, the Church's successful effort to end suicide as an acceptable moral alternative was accomplished by the late fourth century. It was not an issue of widespread philosophical debate and discussion until the rise of twentieth-century existentialism. It has re-entered the popular consciousness only recently, dramatized by Dr. Jack Kevorkian's "suicide machine" and the debate about euthanasia.[34] As such, it has again entered the pastoral concerns of the Churches.

In like manner, numerous particular issues serve to challenge both thought and practice of the Orthodox Church in the post-Soviet period. The shock of having to deal with issues of public concern – if not for the society itself, but for its own membership – for most Churches of the former Soviet block is great.

Numerous issues of popular culture, pastoral goals, and methodologies, assault those Orthodox Churches of the former Soviet block. Some of these, for example, are numerous sexual issues (such as birth control, homosexuality, abortion, venereal diseases, and AIDS), inter-faith marriages, the family, child abuse, divorce, human rights, racism, criminal justice, war and peace, ecology, health and healing, death and dying, and euthanasia. These and numerous other moral and social questions challenge these Churches in a unique way, since in the seventy-year period of Soviet domination it was not possible even to reflect on most of them, much less address them pastorally.[35]

Some of these issues have been placed on the agenda for a forthcoming "Great and Holy Council" of the Orthodox Church and a draft study paper has been prepared on the topic "Peace, Freedom, Brotherhood, and Love," but the paper has not been treated as yet as a public document.[36]

Other topics of concern for the contemporary Orthodox Church which demand attention are Orthodox missions, the place of women in the Church, the tasks of Orthodox theology, and theological education.[37]

THE CHALLENGE OF "CHURCH, NATION, AND FREEDOM"

Together with these and many other issues of the modern

world there is the outstanding concern of the role of the Orthodox Church in the life of the newly-liberated traditionally Orthodox Churches, their relationship with the new political situations that have come into being, and the question of religious
liberty and freedom in these nation-states essentially, the questions provoked by the encounter of the Orthodox described at
the beginning of this paper.

The critical issue is the encounter or juxtaposition of two
apparently contradictory concepts and presuppositions based
on two fundamentally contradictory approaches to human life
and existence. On the one hand is the idea of freedom as understood and promulgated in western democracies, focused primarily on individualism. As had been noted above, much of the
western intellectual tradition understands society as arising from
the primarily reality of the individual.

Modern social and political theory in the West assumes the
primacy of the individual over society. In this context, the exercise of freedom is an individually based right to do whatever
one wants to do. The individual right to choose, to act in an
essentially unrestrained fashion according to that individual
choice, without necessary reference to norms, standards, or transcendent realities, but primarily those subjectively posited by
the moral agent, then became a philosophical definition of existence.

This understanding becomes the working context for the exercise of freedom in much of contemporary philosophy, popular
culture, the United States legal system, and of theological reflection. Of course, the ultimate conclusion of this view is anar-
chy in social life, and so there remain significant limitations to
its full exercise. Increasingly, however, the moral norms, transcendent referents, social institutions, and cultural, biological,
and ethnic limitations to this understanding of freedom are los-
ing their ability to channel freedom understood in such a fashion.[38]

Illustrating this common understanding of freedom is a definition in a well-known dictionary, among which are following

entries: "exemption from external control," "the power to determine action without restraint," and "the absence of or release
from ties or obligations."[39]

This last entry illustrates the individualist character of the
western understanding of freedom. Another tradition, not ab-
sent in the West, but more dominant in the East, is the view
that the individual is the product of social life and that a measure of fullness of life requires both personal inter-relationships
and a social matrix for individual personal identity, growth, and
maturation. "Personal life," which requires relationships with
others, is contrasted with "Individual life," which is essentially
atomistic in character. One finds formation, identity, and
selfhood through involvement in social, cultural, and ethnic
wholes. One's "being" is formed and given content in large part
by these relationships.

In an Eastern Orthodox theological context, what the West
calls, freedom, especially "freedom of choice," is affirmed, but
by more specific nomenclature. The creation of human beings
in the divine image differentiates human beings in significant
ways from the rest of the creation. Among these and deriving
from the Κατ' εἰκόνα and the Καθ' ὁμοίωσιν (Image and Likeness) is "self-determination," or αὐτεξούσιον, which is the human capacity to choose between alternative courses of action,
i.e., to determine one's own behavior. The term "freedom," or
ἐλευθερία is reserved in the patristic tradition for the state or
condition reached in *Theosis*[40] (the fullness of communion with
God that realizes the human potential of God-likeness), "where
there is no conflict or struggle in acting in a fully human, divine-like fashion."[41]

Genuine freedom is teleological and consequently only cor-
porately expressible. To be "free" in this understanding of
ἐλευθεία is a quest of human fulfillment which cannot take
place unrelated to others or without communion with others.
Hence the central Eastern patristic focus on Johannine love. No
one in the Eastern patristic tradition has articulated this more
fully than Maximos the Confessor.[42]

His well-known effort to overcome the five human dichotomies of the human condition is one example that emphasizes integration, communion, and inter-relatedness for full human existence over individualistic understandings. Thus, the saving work of Christ is seen by Maximos as bridging the polarities of uncreated and created nature, intelligible and material creation, heaven and earth, heavenly existence and ordinary life, and between male and female. In the words of Paul Blowers, in Maximos' perspective, "Christ bridges the five polarities and brings the creation into full communion with God." Blowers describes Maximos' achievement as "an abiding paradigm of theology as an integrative and visionary task better yet, as an *integrative vision.*"[43]

When more earth-bound understandings of human identity as formed in and by culture and national identity are brought into relationship with a theology that emphasizes corporate, interpersonal, integrative understandings of human existence, the idea of freedom loses its individualistic tone and assumes the character of "becoming" fully what one really is. It is easier, then, to see how this theologically-based understanding of freedom can and has been put to work in defining "Orthodox peoples" and "Orthodox nations." Within that framework, it becomes readily possible to even come to the point of identifying Orthodoxy with nation (ἔθνος) and "freedom" as accordable to that which contributes to the religious/ethnic identity of the persons who form and are formed by it.

It can and does explain how a modern nation-state like Greece on the one hand affirms the political right of the exercise of religious freedom while adopting Eastern Orthodox Christianity as the official religion of both state and nation. The right to the exercise of one's own religion is protected by law; but overt proselytism is not. This also explains the recent revision, even by a parliament dominated by former communists, of the Freedom of Conscience law in Russia. The recent revision requires the registration of those who have entered the country to proselytize. One reporter described the action with this lectically significant opening paragraph:

> Russia's parliament, heeding warnings from alarmed Or-
> thodox clerics and outraged nationalists, passed a law re-
> cently restricting independent preaching, the seeking of
> converts and religious advertising by foreigners in Rus-
> sia.[44]

While reaction from the West is predictable under those
circumstances, it should not have come as a surprise. In his
Christian Century article "Reviving Religion in the U.S.S.R.,"
published in October of 1990, Jim Forest described the then
developing situation of *perestroika* in the Soviet Union. He wrote:
"Gorbachev's June 12 meeting with (Patriarch) Aleksy indicated
once again the general secretary's awareness that *perestroika's* fate
is bound up with national religious vitality. Seizing the opportunity to press for modification of legislation pending before
the Supreme Soviet, Aleksy asked Gorbachev to back optional
religious education in school. To do otherwise, Aleksy said, would
be "a step back from the development of the democratic process."[45]

Surely, to American ears nothing could be more illustrative
of a differing understanding of freedom and democracy! S. Mark
Heim, a well-known Protestant theologian, reported on his con-
versations with Russians in the same issue of the *Christian Century* as the Jim Forest article. Heim notes that "most Orthodox
find Western warnings of Caesaropapism exaggerated and un-
convincing" in regard to the interests of the Orthodox for vol-
untary choice of religious instruction in the state schools. He
further reported:

> We heard explicit rejection of easy analogies to the U.S.
> experience. Several people told us that while the Ameri-
> can approach to pluralism may be appropriate in a land
> where nearly all citizens came as immigrants from various
> cultures, in a nation with a thousand-year history uniting
> race, culture and religion, this will necessarily and rightly
> be different. Though some of the more dissident Ortho-

dox expressed fears about the manipulation of the church by nationalistic politicians, even they affirmed the special relationship of Russian national identity with Orthodoxy and saw the renewal of this cultural tradition as crucial.[46]

Heim holds that this attitude among the Russians "reflects a genuine Russian nationalism that looks to Orthodoxy like the lost soul of an orphaned culture." I believe that something similar could be said about every traditional national Orthodox Church, even those in the process of coming into existence. It is no accident that a history of early Orthodox presence in the northern part of our hemisphere was titled, *Orthodox America,* reflecting that long-standing incarnational impetus of Orthodox Christianity.[47]

My point in these immediately preceding paragraphs was to highlight differing perceptions about Church and nation and the notions of freedom as it relates to them. I hope that I have made clear why the title of the session described at the beginning of this paper come across as particularly prejudiced to Eastern Orthodox ears.

What is "intolerance" for the Westerner is the denial of being and identity for the Easterner.

ASSUMPTIONS IN NEED OF CORRECTION: TOWARD A NORMATIVE STANCE

Yet, in spite of these affirmations, many problems remain as challenges for the Orthodox in the area of freedom, even within the contexts and understandings that have been just described.

An extremely important dimension of this situation is the tension from within the Orthodox understandings of the relationship of Orthodoxy to both the ethnic and the universal or catholic dimensions of faith. There is an all-too-easy movement from a legitimate "incarnation of the Orthodox Faith in the ethnic cultures of peoples"[48] to submersion of the Faith to ethnic interests – what could be called an "ethno-cultural caesoropapism." Thus, the danger exists for the Gospel of salvation, the integrity of ecclesial life and the catholic vision of the Christian mission to be submerged in the deep waters of religiously sanctioned ethnicism or nationalism.

True, this has been condemned frequently by Orthodox writers, and even by an important Council of the Orthodox Church which dealt with Bulgarian "ethnophyleticism,"[49] yet it remains a thorn in the side of Orthodoxy. The issue was debated with intensity by the late Professor John Karmiris of the University of Athens and Bishop Antonie Plamadeala of Romania at the Second Congress of Orthodox Theological Schools held in Athens in 1976. The former emphasized the primacy of the catholic dimension of the Orthodox Faith, while the latter developed a strong theological stance emphasizing the link between Orthodoxy and ethnicity.[50]

The failures produced by an uncritical and too-close relationship of the Orthodox Church to its ethnic and cultural associations came to the fore precisely during the period of the Soviet Era. Both non-Orthodox and Orthodox critics have documented these failures and what might honestly be called betrayals. Thus, in a recent work, Carnegie Samuel Calian, a Presbyterian scholar and student of Orthodoxy, noted that the Orthodox Church under the Ceausescu regime in Romania was "an example of misapplied *symphonia* eclipsing Orthodoxy's prophetic responsiblility and faithfulness to truth and justice ... In retrospect, it can be seen that the Romanian Orthodox Church ... paid too high a price in its uncritical support of the state."[51]

No one, however, on the American scene has been more critical of the Orthodox Church in these situations than the Orthodox priest and ethicist Alexander F. C. Webster, in his controversial volume, *The Price of Prophecy.* Focusing primarily on the Russian and Romanian Churches in this context, he severely criticizes both Churches for the absence of a sufficiently distanced stance allowing for more ecclesial integrity before the militantly atheistic governments of those two nations. In his forward to Webster's volume, Harvard historian George Hunston Williams describes the work:

> Fr. Webster makes the case that Orthodox leadership has all too often sacrificed true Orthodox ethical principles in failing to act forthrightly (prophetically) under ideologically oppressive, or indifferently secular, governments. His painstaking and comprehensive analysis of the public moral witness of the various Churches on selected issues, set against his identification of the whole range of possible utterances – from courageous prophecy, through prudential evasion, to ignoble propaganda – reveals, alas, that the record of the Orthodox in the twentieth century has been far, far below expectations.[52]

Nevertheless, Webster also notes that others among the Orthodox did exercise prophetic ministries. What perhaps Webster fails to do is not to be fully sensitive to the wide range of methods available to believers in support of the mission of keeping Orthodox Christianity alive in a contrived atmosphere of persecution. Without doubt, there was a "faithful remnant," for whom Orthodox Christianity continued to define its existence and life.

Yet, regardless of what happened in the recent past, it is my contention that the post-Soviet realities in what was formerly Orthodox Eastern Europe are not those that the Orthodox are presently appealing to for justification of a return to the pre-Soviet *status quo*. While the historic connection between the identity of specific peoples and Orthodoxy remains, the present reality – after seventy years of atheistic propaganda, anti-Christian persecution, and the inculcation of Marxist-Leninist ways of thinking – is not what it was. In addition to the "faithful remnant," there are millions of people who may have a vague nostalgia for Orthodoxy or even more diffusely, for "the spirit of their people," which they somehow search to recover. At this point, they can hardly constitute an "Orthodox nation," in a meaningful sense, other than as a reasonable potential to become once again a national embodiment of the Orthodox faith.

Given this personal, pastoral, and national drama, many Orthodox Christians, both within and outside of these nations,

ask if the proselytizing influx of western missionaries is spiritu-
ally and morally justifiable.

Seeking with extremely limited means to re-evangelize their
own peoples, instead of help and cooperation, these Churches
find their work undercut by every manner of proselytizing effort. It is as if the Orthodox Churches and their at least nominal constituencies in these nations are being treated as some
sort of ecclesiastical carrion, to be picked apart while still on
their knees after seventy years of battering by militant atheism.
In the view of the Orthodox, simple human decency in such a
situation would seek rather to assist these fellow Churches in
ministering to their natural constituencies.

I seek for what Ion Bria has called, in another context, "a
time of grace," for the Orthodox Churches to assume their work
in each of these nations, to address their problems and re-evangelize their nations.[53] Needless to say, such a "time of grace"
cannot be limitless, but ethically and morally speaking, the western world should recognize that simple human decency demands
it.

On the part of the Orthodox, however, there must come an
acceptance one day of the truth that the old means of state/
church accommodation will never return. This means that the
means available to the Christian Church are those that it had
available to it in the pre-Constantinian period. Even today, in
Greece, a nation that has an established Orthodox Church, serious discussions about Church-State separation are taking place.
The justification for legalized coercion against non-Orthodox
proselytizers are seen to be less and less supportable, while at
the same time even former left-leaning politicians affirm the
need of the nation to rediscover and re-affirm its Orthodox
Christian roots.[54]

In 1992, Metropolitan Ierotheos of the "Synodical Committee on Heresies" of the Church of Greece reported on the work
of this committee in seeking to counter the effects of proselytizing in Greece. He argues for a vigorous struggle against those
who would draw the people away from their membership in

the Orthodox Church. But the means he calls upon are a return to that tradition of the Church Fathers that focused on teaching, preaching, persuasion, the nurture of faith among the members of the Church, and effective pastoral care.[55]

What is being called for is a broader and more complex understanding of the mission of the Church in the post-Soviet world. This view accepts Azkoul's affirmation that the Church in many ways must remain discontinuous from that which is not Church, so it cannot be *ultimately* identified with any cultural, political reality or ethnic identity. It is in the world but not of the world. Nevertheless, as Guroian reminds us, its mission is to the world, both as a model for life and in a prophetic stance in relationship to the world's sinful dimensions. But, because the Gospel is "for the life of the world" as Khodre and others remind us, at its heart, the Church must be intentionally incarnationally present in whatever is wholesome and in conformity with divine life in the world. None of these dimensions should be confused with the other, but neither should they be subsumed under the other, nor isolated from the others in the mission of the Church. Where separation is required, it should be maintained, where prophetic critique is demanded, it should be offered in love. Always there should be the modeling of God-like life, together with the affirmation and support of those things that are positive and good in that which is formally not Church. Secretly these many good things are the Kingdom already present in the world.

In order to fulfill its mission, the Church must exercise its ministries co-equally and concurrently toward the person, the community of the faithful, and to the world. The nurture of personal growth in the divine image of each member of the Church, in an ascetic process of repentance and renewal, is the *sine qua non* of Church life and outreach to the world. Without souls that love God, there is nothing further that the Church can do. But this is impossible without the personal incorporation of persons into the body of Christ, without the corporate experience of communion with Christ in the Holy Spirit, in worship, sacramental life, and love. But a Church content with being concerned only with its inner life, betrays its Lord who was sent by His heavenly Father into the world for its salvation and redemption. Ecclesiologically, a Church that functions without mission consciousness, without philanthropic care for those who suffer, and without concern for the rectification – as much as is possible in a fallen world – of the systemic evils that pervade it, has betrayed a significant portion of its ministry.

These interpenetrating and mutually enriching dimensions of Church existence can be thoroughly documented in the ongoing tradition of the Orthodox Church, in its monastic, mystical, liturgical, doctrinal, canonical, ethical, missiological, philanthropic, and social experience. This integrated, wholistic vision of Orthodoxy allows for no reductionisms to comfortable patterns into which historical circumstances may have channelled the Orthodox in specific times and places. This *perichoretic* reality, rather, is a continuing challenge to the Orthodox in every age and time, coming directly out its own tradition. The specific needs and demands will vary from one social and historical circumstance to the other. But the challenge of the tradition remains always to confront the Orthodox.[56]

Jaroslav Pelikan begins and ends his book, *The Vindication of Tradition* with a quotation from Goethe. It summarizes the message that the Orthodox must hear and respond to in the post-Soviet period:

> What you have as heritage,
> Take now as task;
> For thus you will make it your own.[57]

This return to earlier traditions for Orthodoxy must also mean a renewed respect for freedom and a stronger commitment to the method of persuasion and spiritual example, on what should be a level playing field. There is a case to be made for a return by the contemporary Orthodox Church to an early Church and patristic commitment to freedom that respects fully the self-determining αὐτεξούσιον of every human being. This is a commitment to the "Voices of Religious Liberty in the Early

Church," as expressed the title of an article by Everett Ferguson.[58]

In that article, passages from early Church writings provide what seem to be very contemporary and modern perspectives, that need to inspire the Orthodox to a renewed understanding of mission and ministry in the new millennium that is dawning upon it. With some of these early Christian judgments on religious freedom, I will conclude this paper.

From Tertullian:

> It is a fundamental human right, a privilege of nature, that every man should worship according to his own convictions: one man's religion neither harms nor helps another man. It is assuredly no part of religion to compel religion – to which free will and not force should lead us (*Scapula,* 2).[59]

> Religion is to be defended, not by putting to death, but by dying; not by cruelty, but by patient endurance; not by guilt, but by good faith ... For if you wish to defend religion by bloodshed, and by tortures, and by guilt, it will no longer be defended, but will be polluted and profaned. For nothing is much a matter of free-will as religion. *(Divine Institutes,* 20).[60]

From the Edict of Milan:

> It seemed to us that, amongst those things that are profitable to mankind in general, the reverence paid to the Divinity merited our first and chief attention, and that it was proper that the Christians and all others should have liberty to follow that mode of religion which each of them appeared best... (Lactantius, *On the Deaths of the Persecutors,* 48)[61]

From St. Athanasius:

> The truth is not preached with swords or with darts, nor by means of soldiers; but by persuasion and counsel. But what persuasion is there where fear of the Emperor prevails? Or what counsel is there, when he who withstands

them receives at last banishment and death? *(Apology for His Flight,* 23); and

For it is part of true godliness not to compel, but to persuade *(History of the Arians,* 33:67).[62]

From St. John Chrysostom:

It ill befits Christians of all men to correct the mistakes of the erring by constraint. Judges without the Christian fold may exercise coercion against those who are legally convicted, but in our case such men must be brought to a better fruit, by persuasion rather than by compulsion. The laws do not confer upon us authority of this sort for coercing the delinquent, nor if they did confer upon us authority of this sort for coercing the delinquent, nor if they did could we use it, because God crowns those who refrain from evil by choice and not by necessity ... The priest has much to do also in gathering up the scattered members of the church. The shepherd can recall a wandering sheep with a shout, but if a man errs from the true faith, the pastor has need of great effort, perseverance, and patience. The wanderer cannot be dragged by force or constrained by fear. Only persuasion can restore him to the truth from which he has fallen away *(On the Priesthood,* II:3,4).[63]

ENDNOTES

*This paper is a revised version of my presentation "Challenges to Orthodoxy" given at the Loyola Marymount University - Los Angeles Conference on "Crisis of Cultures and Birth of Faith" on September 25, 1993 as part of Session V. "Church vs. State or Religious Freedom vs. Intolerance." The version presented in the proceedings of the conference was published in *Formulation of Christianity by Conflict through the Ages.* Lewiston, ME: Edwin Mellen Press, 1995.
[1] Ἡ Ζ' Γενική Συνέλευσις τοῦ Παγκοσμίου Συμβουλίου Ἐκκλησιῶν. Καμπέρρα, Φεβρουάριο 1991. Χρονικόν, Κείμενα, Ἀξιολογήσεις (The 7th General Assembly of the World

Council of Churches: Canberra, February, 1991: Chronicle, Texts, Evaluations). (Katerine, Greece: "TERTIOS" Publications), pp. 71-77.

[2]*Faith Gives Fullness to Reasoning: The Five Theological Orations of Gregory of Nazianzen.* Introduction and Commentary by Fredrick W. Norris. Tr. by Lionel Wickham and Frederick Williams. (New York: E. J. Brill, 1991).

[3]Thomas Guarino, "Between Foundationalism and Nihilism: Is *Phronesis* the *Via Media* for Theology?" *Theological Studies,* 54 (1953), pp. 37-54. In his conclusions, Guarino answers his title question in the negative, thus remaining committed to the rational foundationalism of the West.

[4] "The Sacramental Life of the Orthodox Church," in *A Companion to the Greek Orthodox Church.* Ed. Fotios K. Litsas. (New York: Department of Communication: Greek Orthodox Archdiocese of North and South America, 1984), p. 31.

[5]Alexander Schmemann, *Introduction to Liturgical Theology,* tr. Asheleigh E. Moorehouse, (Portland, ME: American Orthodox Press, 1966).

[6]*7th General Assembly,* p. 69.

[7]James J. Stamoolis, *Eastern Orthodox Mission Theology Today.* No. 10 in the American Society of Missiology Series. (Maryknoll, NY: Orbis Books, 1986), p. 61. Stamoolis' Chapter VIII, "The Method of Mission," is a useful introduction to the theory of the practice of mission in Orthodox theology.

[8]Max Weber, *The Protestant Ethic and the Spirit of Capitalism.* (New York: Charles Scribner's Sons, 1930); Ephraim Fischoff, "The Protestant Ethic and the Spirit of Capitalism, the History of a Controversy," *Social Research,* XI, pp. 53-77.

[9]L. William Countryman, *The Rich Christian in the Church of the Early Empire: Contradictions and Accommodations* (New York: The Edwin Mellen Press, 1980).

[10]Peter C. Phan, *Social Thought,* vol. 20 of "The Message of the Fathers of the Church." (Wilmington, DE: Michael Glazier, Inc., 1984).

[11]Phan, p. 42.

[12]Robert N. Bellah, *et al, Habits of the Heart: Individualism and Commitment in American Life,* (New York: Harper & Row, 1986); _____, *The Good Society,* (New York: Knopf, 1992).

[13]Demetrios J. Constantelos, *Issues and Dialogues in the Orthodox Church Since World War Two*. (Brookline, MA: Holy Cross Orthodox Press, 1991), p. 26.

[14]See my articles, "The Orthodox Theological Approach to Modern Trends," *St. Vladimir's Theological Quarterly*. Vol. 13, No. 4, (1969), pp. 198-211; "The Church and the Secular World," *Greek Orthodox Theological Review*. Vol. XVII, Spring, (1972), No. 1; "Greek Orthodox Ethics and Western Ethics," *Journal of Ecumenical Studies*. Vol. 10, No. 4, Fall, (1973), pp. 728-751; "The Meaning of the Adaption of Orthodoxy to the Contemporary World," *Epistemonike Epiteris*. The University of Thessalonike, School of Theology. Vol. 19, (1974), pp. 127-140; "Reflections on the Ethical Dimensions of the Topics of the Great and Holy Synod," *Greek Orthodox Theological Review*. Vol. 24, Summer/Fall (1979), pp. 131-157; "Foundations of Orthodox Christian Social Vision," *Diakonia*. Vol XVIII, No. 2, 1983; "Orthodoxy In America: Continuity, Discontinuity, Newness," Theodore Stylianopoulos, ed., *Orthodox Perspectives on Pastoral Practice*. Brookline, MA: Holy Cross Orthodox Press, 1988, pp. 13-29.

[15]Much of that which follows on the three authors is based on a paper of mine presented at my home institution, Holy Cross Greek Orthodox School of Theology, at a "Theological Symposium on Faith and Culture In Honor of Archbishop Iakovos' 38th Anniversary as Primate of the Greek Orthodox Archdiocese." The conference was held in Brookline, Massachusetts, April 23-25, 1990. The title of my paper is "Faith and Culture in Contemporary Orthodox Theology." The full text was published in the 1991 volume of *The Greek Orthodox Theological Review*.

[16]*St. Vladimir's Theological Quarterly*, Vol. 23, No. 1, 1979, pp. 3-21 and Vol. 23, No. 2, pp. 67-86.

[17]For example, one of his many works on the subject is *Towards A Christian Civilization*. (Athens: Damascus Press, 1955).

[18] "The Greek Fathers," *St. Vladimir's Seminary Quarterly*, vol. 23, no. 1, p. 5.

[19]Azkoul, p. 13.

[20]Azkoul, p. 86.

[21]Ernst Troeltsch, *The Social Teachings of the Christian Churches*. 2 vols. Tr. Olive Wyon. (New York: Macmillan Co., 1931).

[22]Vigen Guroian, *Incarnate Love: Essays In Orthodox Ethics*, (Notre

Dame, IN: University of Notre Dame Press 1987).

[23]His views are primarily expressed in the fifth and sixth chapters, "The Problem of a Social Ethic: Diaspora Reflections," and "Orthodoxy and American Order: Symphonia, Civil Religion or What?" Guroian has since significantly expanded his purview in his second book on Ethics, in which a more positive role for the Church in the world begins to emerge, *Ethics after Christendom: toward an ecclesial Christian ethic.* Grand Rapids, MI: Eerdmans Pub. Co., 1994. His work focusing on his own Armenian Orthodox Church is both prophetic-critical and constructive: *Faith, church, mission: essays for renewal in the Armenian Church.* New York: Armenian Prelacy, 1995. In the same mode, critical, but even more constructive and outreaching is his work on death and dying, *Life's living toward dying: a theological and medical-ethical study.* Grand Rapids, MI: W.B. Eerdmans Pu. Co., 1996. Perhaps his study of how children's literature serves in the formation of character is most positive, in that it has been characterized as a "guide ... through some of the best literature for children, especially with an eye towards the moral and religious significance of those stories": *Tending the heart of virtue: how classic stories awaken a child's moral imagination.* New York: Oxford University Press, 1998.

[24]Alexander Webster, *The Price of Prophesy: Orthodox Churches on Peace, Freedom, and Security,* (Washington, DC: Ethics and Public Policy Center, 1993). Some aspects of Webster's work will be discussed below.

[25]Guroian, p. 148.

[26]"The Church and the World," *St. Vladimir's Theological Quarterly.* vol. 13, 1969, nos. 1-2, pp. 33-51.

[27]Khodre p. 37.

[28]Khodre, p. 47.

[29]Khodre, p. 50.

[30]Ephesians 1.16-23.

[31]I refer the reader to my discussion of the term "world" in its several understandings in the tradition and as it relates to Orthodox Ethics in the article, "The Church and the Secular World," *Greek Orthodox Theological Review.* Vol. XVII, Spring, (1972), No. 1.

[32]2 Timothy 4.17.

[33]Philippians 4.8.

[34]See Elias Boulgarakes, 1992, *Αὐτοκτονία καὶ Ἐκκλησιαστικὴ*

Ταφή, (Suicide and Ecclesiastical Burial), (Athens: Armos Publications, 1992); John Breck, 1988 "Bio-Medical Technology: Of the Kingdom or of the Cosmos?" St. *Vladimir's Theological Quarterly,* vol. 32, 1988, no. 1, pp. 5-26); _____, "Selective Nontreatment of the Terminally Ill: An Orthodox Moral Perspective," *St. Vladimir's Theological Quarterly,* vol. 33, 1989, no. 3, 261-273); Stanley S. Harakas, "The Greek Orthodox Church" and Thomas Hopko, "The Orthodox Church in America" in G. A. Larue, (ed.): *Euthanasia and Religion: A Survey of the Attitudes of World Religions to the Right to Die* (Los Angeles: The Hemlock Society, 1985, pp. 45-56, 55-57); Athenagoras N. Zakopoulos, Ἡ Ἀθανασία Σήμερα καὶ ἡ Θέση τῆς Ἐκκλησίας (Euthanasia Today and the Position of the Church) (Athens: Diakonia of the Church of Greece, 1987).

[35]For a brief treatment of these and other similar issues from an Orthodox perspective, see Stanley S. Harakas, *Contemporary Moral Issues Facing the Orthodox Christian.* (Minneapolis, MN: Light and Life Publishing Co., 1982). See also, by the same author: *For the Health of Body and Soul: An Eastern Orthodox Introduction to Bioethics,* (Brookline, MA: Holy Cross Orthodox Press, 1980); 'The Stand of the Orthodox Church on Controversial Issues,' in *A Companion to the Greek Orthodox Church,* (New York: Greek Orthodox Archdiocese, 1984); *Health and Medicine in the Eastern Orthodox Tradition,* (New York: Crossroad Publishing Co., NY, 1990). For a bibliography of Orthodox reflections on bioethical issues, see Stanley S. Harakas "Eastern Orthodox" in Lustig, B. A., ed. *Theological Developments in Bioethics: 1988-1990, Bioethics Yearbook: Volume 1,* (Dordrect, Netherlands: Kluwer Academic Publishers, 1991), pp. 85-101. "Eastern Orthodox," Lustig, A.C. ed. *Theological Developments in Bioethics: 1990-1992: Volume 3* [Dordrect, Netherlands: Kluwer Academic Publishers, 1991], pp. 117-132.

[36]Stanley S. Harakas, *Something is Stirring in World Orthodoxy: An Introduction to the Forthcoming Great and Holy Council of the Eastern Orthodox Church.* (Minneapolis, MN: Light and Life Publishing Co., 1978).

[37]A short list of references to Orthodox reflection on these topics follows:

Missions: Ion Bria, *Martyria/Mission,* (Geneva: World Council of Churches Press, 1980; Francis Dvornik, *Byzantine Missions Among the Slavs,* (New Brunswick: Rutgers University Press, 1970); Aram Keshishian, *Orthodox Perspectives on Mission,* (Oxford: Regnum Books, 1992); Paul Garrett, *St. Innocent, Apostle to America,* (Crestwood, NY: St. Vladimir's Seminary Press, 1978); Michael J. Oleksa, *Alaskan Missionary Spirituality* (Mahwah, NJ: Paulist Press, 1987); *Orthodox Alaska: A Theology of Mission,(Crestwood,* NY: St. Vladimir's Seminary Press, 1992); Alexander Schmemann, *Church, World, Mission,* (Crestwood, NY: St. Vladimir's Seminary Press, 1979); James J. Stamoolis, *Eastern Orthodox Missionary Theology Today,* (Maryknoll, NY: Orbis Books, 1986).

Women: For contemporary reflection on the topic of Women in the Orthodox Church together with an extensive bibliography, see *The Place of Woman in the Orthodox Church and the Question of the Ordination of Women: InterOrthodox Symposium, Rhodos, Greece, 30 October-7 November, 1988.* Ed., Gennadios Limouris (Katerine, Greece: "Tertios" Publications, 1992).

Theological Education: An interesting successful example of the struggle to address theological education in a formerly communist governed "Orthodox nation" is Ion Bria's article "Orthodox Theological Education: The Case of Romania," in *Ministerial Formation,* 61, April, 1993, pp. 26-33.

[38]For a discussion of existentialism in ethics, that informs the preceding paragraphs, see my book, *Toward Transfigured Life: The "Theoria" of Eastern Orthodox Ethics* (Minneapolis, MN: Light and Life Publishing Co, 1983), pp. 59-65. For an effort that seeks to incorporate existentialist perspectives into Orthodox theology, see Christos Yannaras, *The Freedom of Ethos,* tr. Elizabeth Briere,(Crestwood, NY: St. Vladimir's Seminary Press, 1984). The view expressed in the preceding paragraphs has been informed, also, by the seminal work of Robert N. Bellah, *Habits of the Heart.*

[39]*Random House Webster's College Dictionary,* (New York: Random House, 1991).

[40]For a treatment of "Theosis" or "Deification" or "Divinization" in the Orthodox tradition, see, in order of descending complexity: Vladimir Lossky, *The Mystical Theology of the Eastern Church,* (London: James Clarke & Co., 1957); Georgios Mantzaridis, *The Deification of Man: St. Gregory Palamas and the Orthodox Tradition,* tr. Liadain Sherrard, (Crestwood, NY: St. Vladimir's Seminary Press, 1984);

Christoforos Stavropoulos, *Partakers of Divine Nature,* tr. Stanley S. Harakas,(Minneapolis, MN: Light and Life Publishing Co., 1976).

[41]Stanley S. Harakas, *Toward Transfigured Life,* p. 34.

[42]Lars Thunberg, *Man and the Cosmos: The Vision of St. Maximus the Confessor* (Crestwood, NY: St. Vladimir's Seminary Press, 1985).

[43]Paul M. Blowers, "Theology as Integrative, Visionary, Pastoral: The Legacy of Maximus the Confessor," *Pro Ecclesia,* vol. II, Spring, 1993, no. 2, pp. 225, 217.

[44]John-Thor Dahlburg, "Russia Puts Restrictions on Outside Religions." *Hellenic Chronicle,* LXXXVI, no. 6, Aug. 12, 1993.

[45]Jim Forest, "Reviving Religion in the U.S.S.R," *The Christian Century,* October 10, 1990, p. 905.

[46]S. Mark Heim, "Without Czar or Commissar: Church and Nation in Russia," *The Christian Century,* October 10, 1990, p. 909.

[47]*Orthodox America 1794-1976,* Constance T. Tarasar, ed. (Syosett, NY: Orthodox Church in America, 1975).

[48]George Every, "Dvornik on National Churches," *Eastern Churches Review,* vol IX, 1977, pp. 17-25, in which Francis Dvornik's 1944 book, *National Churches and the Church Universal* is treated at length and in which a defense of national churches is developed by a highly respected Roman Catholic historian.

[49]The Bulgarian Schism of the 19th Century was addressed by an Orthodox "Great Council" held in Constantinople August 29 to September 17, 1872, which condemned the effort of that Church to define itself in ethnic categories, in which the national identity overwhelmed the Orthodox ecclesial identity. According to Orthodox Church historian B. Stephanides the error which was condemned by the Council "consisted primarily in that they sought to form their own independent Church... only on the basis of ethnic differentiation, which was characterized by the Great Council as *"ethnophyleticism."* in Ἐκκλησιαστική Ἱστορία Ἀπ' ἀρχῆς μέχρι Σήμερον, (Athens: Aster Publishing House, 1948), p. 681.

[50]For a first-hand report of the debate, see Kallistos Ware, "Catholicity and Nationalism: A Recent Debate at Athens," *Eastern Churches Review,* vol IX, 1977, pp. 10-16. The full text of this interesting exchange can be found in *Proces - Verbaux du Deuxieme Congres de Theologie Orthodoxe a Athenes 19-29 Aut 1976,* ed. Savas C. Agourides, (Athens, 1978), pp. 458-518.

[51]Carnegie Samuel Calian, *Theology Without Boundaries: Encounters of Eastern Orthodoxy and Western Tradition,* (Louisville: Westminster/ John Knox Press, 1992), p.73.

[52]*The Price of Prophecy,* pp. xiii-xiv.

[53]Speaking of the faithful and the clergy of the Romanian Orthodox Church who are committed to renewal, Fr. Bria says, "They are preparing for the day of complete deliverance, they are looking for a time of grace." "Orthodox Theological Education," p. 26.

[54]Numerous papers espousing various aspects of this concern were delivered at a Greek Parliament sponsored conference held at Ormylia of the province of Chalkidike, June 30 to July 4, 1993. The conference title was "Orthodoxy in the New European Reality."

[55] Μητρ. Ὕδρας, Σπετσῶν καί Αἰγίνης κ. Ἱερόθεος, "Τό Σημερινόν Σκηνικόν τῶν Αἱρέσεων καί τό ἔναντι αὐτῶν χρέος τῆς Ἐκκλησίας" (The Contemporary Scene of the Heresies and the Responsibility of the Church Toward Them), Γρηγόριος Παλαμᾶς 75, 741 Jan-Feb 1992, pp. 21-38.

[56]For a theological understanding of Holy Tradition in contemporary Orthodox theology, see Stanley S. Harakas' review article, "'Tradition' in Eastern Orthodox Thought," *Christian Scholars Review,* xxii:2, December, 1992, pp. 144-165.

[57]Jaroslav Pelikan, *The Vindication of Tradition* (New Haven: Yale University Press, 1984), dedication page and page 82. For the Orthodox, a more literal translation of the first line might be even more meaningful: "Was du ererbt von deinen *Vatern* hast ..." ("What you have inherited from your *Fathers* ...") My emphasis.

[58]Everett Ferguson, "Voices of Religious Liberty in the Early Church," *Restoration Quarterly,* vol. 119, no. 1, 1976, pp. 13-22.

[59]Ferguson, p. 19.

[60]Ferguson, p. 20.

[61]Ferguson, p. 20.

[62]Ferguson, p. 21.

[63]Ferguson, p. 21.

11

Eastern Orthodox Ethics and Community Ethics[*]

Introduction

To reflect on the "ethics of community"[1] is a provocation to define terms. The term "community" has a fairly clear focus. It certainly goes beyond the individual and it is normally distinguished from both the "family," and from the "nation-state." It is located, it would seem, in the sphere between the individual and the family on the one side and the nation-state, and the international sphere on the other side. To speak of community in this sense is to locate it in the important nexus of the lives of people as they intersect with others in the realm just beyond their intimate familial and ecclesial existence, and prior to the more impersonal institutions of the larger society and the nation.

The ethical implications of "community" are wide-ranging. The spheres where "community" is experienced and lived out are located in activities such as public education, private education, public funding, public decorum, private freedoms, sex education, hunger, homelessness, criminal justice, the death penalty, and organized lawlessness. Its purview could also include issues related to ecology, urban design and architecture, and transportation. It could concern itself, as well, with group ethos and pluralism, with substance abuse and economic and corporate ethics.

In short, "ethical issues of community" as a topic speaks to

122

the immediate social environment in which we find ourselves, our families, and our Church and parish lives. It raises the questions of what is permissible and what is not acceptable in the neighborhood, in the public relationships in which we live much of our lives, and in general, in our direct inter-relatedness with others. This paper approaches the sphere of "community" as defined in this manner from the specific perspectives of Orthodox Christian ethics.

Thus, Orthodox Christians live not only in their personal inner worlds and the close environments of family and ethnic and Church communities, but also in this broader environment of "community" as defined above. How is the Orthodox Christian to understand and deal with these spheres which are personally experienced but non-family, non-Church, and distinct from the specific cultural/ethnic traditions in which they have been raised? Stated more broadly, how should we understand the issue of how persons with specific cultural and religious identities understand and engage with "communities" outside their immediate defining identities? Can Orthodox ethics provide some understanding and guidance?

There is a fairly clear vision of the roots and foundations of Orthodox Christian ethics in the Orthodox Christian theological tradition. But it would seem that nearly all of the other issues are riddled with tensions, paradoxes, and with many dilemmas.

In discussing the issue of the Eastern Orthodox Christian understanding of community ethics, then, this essay will speak briefly about some of the theological perspectives which lead to Orthodox Christian approaches to community, first in its ecclesial and then extra-ecclesial dimensions. Subsequently, since this reflection on the ethics of "community" is treated as a phenomenon of American life, I intend to address briefly eight dilemmas which face this country, proposing some Eastern Orthodox responses to them. Consequently, this effort treats the question of community on the level of decision-making regarding policy and *praxis*. It seeks to relate foundations with the empirical social realities that form the contemporary context of our experience as Orthodox Christians living in a predominately non-Orthodox cultural setting. What follows below is an effort to do ethics in the realm of the possible.

ANALYSIS AND THEOLOGICAL FOUNDATIONS

There is, in our time, even among those who reject the traditional values of Western civilization and their Christian roots, a sense that we live in a time of decadence. There are many analyses which seek to pinpoint the problem. The liberal tradition, for example, can point to the prostitution of education in the service of career training rather than educating of the mind, as Allan Bloom did in his simultaneously acclaimed and criticized volume *The Closing of the American Mind*. The sub-title of this book accurately describes his charge against American education: *How Higher Education Failed Democracy and Impoverished the Souls of Today's Students*.[2]

From the perspective of the Christian tradition, the answer in general terms to this decadence is that the source of true human values is God; the denial of God and His will for humanity is the chief source of failure and misery in life. As Proverbs long ago put it, "There is a way which seems right to a man but its end is the way to death" (Prov. 14.12).[3] There is a differentiation between the revelatory truth and "earthly wisdom" (2 Cor. 1.12). "This wisdom is not such as comes down from above, but is earthly, unspiritual, devilish" (Jas. 11.15). It may "have indeed an appearance of wisdom" (Col. 2.23), but it is in contrast to the truth "of Christ in whom are hid all the treasures of wisdom and knowledge" (Col. 2. 3).

Further, there is a moral coherence in life according to which consequences fit our choices and behaviors. The New Testament teaches that the servants of evil may "disguise themselves as servants of righteousness;" nevertheless, "their end will correspond to their deeds" (2 Cor. 11.15). In contrast, "spiritual wisdom and understanding" are capable of leading one to "a life worthy of the Lord, fully pleasing to him, (and) bearing fruit in every good work" (Col. 1.9,10). Thus, we are instructed to "Look carefully then how you walk, not as unwise men but as wise, making the most of the time, because the days are evil" (Eph. 5.15-16).

Nowhere is this required more fully than in the disintegrated condition of community in western technological society. At the heart of this situation is a degenerate egotism and self-centeredness. Our age's crooner, Frank Sinatra, boasts, "I did it MY way." We teach everyone to "be themselves" without reference to others or to God. Every gender, race, nationality, class, and profession asserts "rights" against all others, but few couple these claims with the articulation of duties and responsibilities toward others. No wonder there is a sense of deterioration and decadence.

There is not much hope either. As long as twenty years ago researcher John Calhoun was described in the *Smithsonian* magazine as comparing our society with overcrowded rats in mock cities. He attributed to overpopulation the result, which the article described in these words:

> It's not a pretty sight. Some rats hover around the edges of the society, shivering and withdrawn. Homosexuality, cannibalism, and extreme withdrawal occur more and more frequently. The rats even appear to despair of life. Not a very pleasant prediction. But also not a very bad picture of our world living in depressing darkness...[4]

It is precisely this worldview which the comedian Woody Allen espouses and promotes in his movies. He is reported as saying once, "My life is at a crossroads. One path leads to despair and utter hopelessness, and the other to total extinction. I only pray I have the wisdom to choose correctly."[5]

But it is not overpopulation that is the cause of the western world's hopelessness and its crisis of community. There are numerous cultures of the world where populations are much denser than in Europe and America, in spite of which community life

is strong and vigorous. Our decadence is to be found in an ideology which atomizes us, draws us out of communion with God
and our fellows into a privatized, other-rejecting selfishness.[6]
This age is experiencing the fruits of a popularized existentialist
worldview that sees the "other" as enemy and stranger. This is a
way of thinking and valuing which counts as normative a person's
withdrawal from communion with others. It is a search of a
world striving for a distorted self-fulfillment and a false self-
realization, which in its very isolation and avarice is a perver-
sion of what it means to be human. In 1985 a financier stood
before the graduates at a University of California commencement and told them, "Greed is all right ...greed is healthy. You
can be greedy and still feel good about yourself." When he acted
on his beliefs, Ivan Boesky was tried for criminal acts, convicted,
jailed and only recently released. Society, it seems, still has re-
tained some sense of community, but it is in dangerously short
supply.[7]

What has all this to do with Orthodox theology? If it is correct that the source of every true value and true understanding
is God, as the Christian revelation affirms; and if it is a truth
that human existence is created in the image and likeness of
God, as Scripture and Holy Tradition affirm; then it follows
inexorably that human existence finds its meaning and fullness
in the reality of God. In the Orthodox faith tradition it is emphasized repeatedly that the first knowledge human beings have
of God is through the experience of the Triune nature of God as
Father, Son, and Holy Spirit. God is not a unitary abstraction,
though God is one. God is not merely a starting point for a
theological argument. God is not merely a principle for our
thought. God is not merely and idea, a concept, an impersonal
"Prime Mover," or a rational construct. God is a community of
divine persons. Consequently, the truth about God is central
for our understanding of "community."

According to Orthodox theology, God meets humanity as a
Trinity of persons. That is human experience, whether in the
creation, or in the Scripture, or in the Tradition, or in personal

daily existence. Human beings meet the Creator, the Redeemer, and the Sanctifier on the level of personal encounter. In this experience, humanity discovers that the Father is a person; that the Son is a person; that the Holy Spirit is a person. Yet, the three persons – the Holy Trinity – are one God. That affirmation, too, inexorably leads human reflection to the understanding that ultimate reality, God, is a community of persons in His very being and existence.

It is in the image of that God – the God who is a community of persons – that human beings are created. To realize even the most elementary dimensions of our humanity in our empirical existence means that somehow we must be in communion with "others;" with God, with family, with neighbor, with associates on every level of human interaction. Community is an essential dimension of human existence.

The ancient Latin Christian judgment, "*Unus Christianus, nullus Christianus*" (a single, isolated Christian is no Christian at all) is true of Christians. It is also translatable to ordinary human existence: "A single, isolated person, is no person at all." The Greek word for person is πρόσωπον (prosopon). The first part of that word, πρὸς (*pros*) means "to direct one's self toward something." The second part of the word "prosopon" comes from the Greek noun ὄψις (*opsis*) based on a verb which means "to look." A person, by definition, is one who looks, face to face, towards another and communicates with the other. On the campus of the Hellenic College and Holy Cross Greek Orthodox School of Theology, Brookline, Massachusetts, where I teach, there is a larger than life statue of the founder of the School, the late Ecumenical Patriarch Athenagoras. On the base of the statue is an inscription which summarizes the great man's philosophy of life: "Come, let us look into each other's eyes." These words are illustrative of what Orthodox theology understands to be essential for human living. It is the communion of persons in community and relationships.

But the Holy Trinity is not a chaotic relationship, neither is it haphazard, unordered, without structure or pattern. The great theological conflicts between Eastern Christianity and Western Christianity had as one of their major theological themes, the doctrine of the "*Filioque.*" This Latin addition to the Nicene-Constantinopolitan Creed appended the words "and the Son" to the biblical affirmation that the Holy Spirit "proceeds from the Father" (John 15.26).[8] What is important about this dispute in this context is that the Eastern Orthodox insisted on the Scriptural definition of a specific and concrete order, structure, and pattern to the relationship of the three persons of the Holy Trinity in communion. The Father is the source of divinity; the Son is ever born of the Father; the Holy Spirit forever proceeds from the Father. This orderly structure is just as much a part of the relationship of community in the being of God as is the inter-personal communion of love among the three persons of the Holy Trinity.

According to the Fourth Gospel, the same Jesus who affirmed that "I and the Father are one" (John 10.30), and that "the Father loves me" (John 10.17), prays in His great "High-priestly prayer" in John 17 that His followers also share in this relationship. Regarding His disciples, Jesus prays "Holy Father, keep them in thy name, which thou hast given me, that they may be one, even as we are one" (John 17.11, KJV). But nevertheless, this relationship is not a haphazard one. Thus, Jesus is reported as saying in the same Gospel, "Truly, truly, I say to you, a servant is not greater than his master; nor is he who is sent greater than he who sent him" (John 13.16).

There is one more link that has to be noted. It is true that all these words, and, many more like them, are spoken of the disciples and of the Church by Jesus. They do not seem to take into consideration the non-ecclesial communities, which are outside the boundaries of the Church. These passages, at first glance, may appear to exclude the structures of society and the communities which are found in them. Nevertheless, this is not the case. The Church, in its full and appropriate embodiment of community, is a model for that which is non-Church. The Church is in its very existence is an instruction and a guide for the world. Thus, in the same "High-priestly prayer" in John 17, Jesus is reported as praying:

> that they may all be one; even as thou, Father, art in me, and I in thee, that they also may be in us, *so that the world may believe that thou hast sent me.* The glory which thou hast given me I have given to them, that they may be one even as we are one, I in them and thou in me, that they may become perfectly one, *so that the world may know* that thou hast sent me and hast loved them even as thou hast loved me" (John 17.21-23 KJV).

The outcome of this theological reasoning is that if "God so loved the world that he gave his only-begotten Son" (John 3.16) for its salvation, it follows that the model of communion in the Holy Trinity which is to be realized in the Church, is also, after a fashion, a model for the world as a whole, fallen and distorted as it may be. The conclusion is that human community, in a limited, distorted, incomplete, and imperfect way, needs to reflect some of the inter-personal, intimate and yet, at the same time, the ordered and patterned structure of the inner life of the Holy Trinity. Otherwise it cannot be community, and in failing that, it makes impossible the realization of even elemental human existence.

Thus, even non-ecclesial communities participate in some measure in the life of the Trinity. For failing that, the only consequence can be dissolution and destruction. In its most simple form, this is reflected in the conformity or not of a given community to the most elemental, yet essential standard of community living, the Decalogue. For the Greek Fathers, the Decalogue is an elemental, essential, ordering of human society.[9] It is not an externally imposed law, but a description in the creation itself of what holds any given society or community together, giving it the coherence and the structure necessary for it to exist. It is an elemental, basic, low-level ethic for community living.

We have thus come to the kinds of ethical issues included in

the topic "community ethics." These issues, however, do not
come in simple form. They come in the form, rather, of a series
of dilemmas. I propose in the balance this essay, to sketch out
these dilemmas, and at the same time to indicate some Orthodox responses to each. These responses are often articulated in
the form of paradoxes, which seek to hold together apparently
contradictory positions in a whole that transcends their contrasts. This wholistic approach raises the elements of the paradox up to a larger and more inclusive integration, similar to the
way the doctrine of the Holy Trinity unites in One, the Three
Divine persons.[10]

Thus, what follows is modeled after the ecclesial implications
of community, but much of it can be seen as also applicable to
community in the context of the world.

Dilemma I: Education and Formation of Community

In a striking and sobering passage, Allen Siegel points out
what is at stake in the way a society educates its children for
community living. He writes: "When it comes to rearing children, every society is only 20 years away from barbarism. Twenty
years is all we have to accomplish the task of civilizing the in-
fants who are born into our midst each year. These savages know
nothing of our language, our culture, our religion, our values,
our customs of interpersonal relations. The infant is totally ig-
norant about communism, fascism, democracy, civil liberties,
the rights of the minority as contrasted with the prerogatives of
the majority, respect, decency, honesty, customs, conventions,
and manners. The barbarian must be tamed if civilization is to
survive."[11]

There is, however, another side to education. It is the need
to educate for creativity, as well. In an age of rapid change, of
constant innovation and invention, an age when boundaries
change on a daily basis, when culture itself is in flux, it is not
enough to remain embedded in the past.

To press too heavily in education on the side of the communication of inherited values is to form persons rooted in tradition, but incapable of freedom and innovation and creativity. To press too heavily on the subjective self and its creative processes is precisely to bring into being an age where there is no culture to form a matrix for community living.

The socialist nations, with their monopoly of state education had created an educational system of ideological slogan repeating. In such a system youths learn languages readily and expertly, they have strong knowledge of mathematics and the sciences. Their content-oriented education has been an embarrassment to the American educational establishment.

In the western nations, and in particular in the United States, this embarrassment is accentuated by the frequently reported decline of knowledge on the part of students in areas such as elementary English grammar, geography, mathematics, and almost total ignorance of foreign languages and history. Western education, in its Dewey-inspired tradition, earns a plus, though, in self-expression, creativity, freedom, and enterprise.

It seems that both systems, pushed to their logical conclusions are failures. An educational system must effectively communicate the inherited tradition, but yet allow that inherited tradition to function in creative freedom. This is the very essence of the Eastern Orthodox understanding of Tradition as it pertains to the Christian faith. Tradition is not, as is sometimes charged by those outside the Orthodox Church, a blind repetition of the past. Tradition itself is a dynamic reality, which includes within it a freedom which is not chaotic or disoriented, but which is creative and renewing and ordered.

Bishop Hanson, an Anglican theologian, expressed this approach to tradition well. He wrote, "As we study the Fathers (of the Church) we conduct a dialogue with them, putting questions to them and seeing what sort of answers they give, just as they themselves in a sense conducted a dialogue with the Bible. We accept them as partners in the same work as that in which we are engaged, but at a much earlier period of its development..."[12] Education, in order to be genuine, needs to affirm both sides of the equation in a single process which incorporates solid knowledge of the accumulated inheritance of culture and community, together with the searching and inquisitive and creative discovery and forward looking uses of newly acquired knowledge.

It follows that what passes for *public education* in much of urban America accomplishes little of these goals. Yet, public education in a democratic society such as ours seems to be an absolutely necessary institution in order to create and maintain a sense of cohesion and shared fundamental values in a diverse multi-cultural, multi-religious, multiethnic society such as that of the U.S.A. In an earlier time, a too heavy-handed educational system sought to impose what was a White/Anglo-Saxon/Protestant culture upon all that entered the nation. It succeeded in this until it was overwhelmed by internal secularist changes on the one hand and the appearance of too many diverse cultural, racial, religious, and ethnic groups on the other.

One answer to this state of affairs was the development *of private education,* first appearing in the parochial school system of the Roman Catholic Church and, in the present day, in the "Christian Academies" of conservative and fundamentalist Protestantism. There are also small numbers of private schools of other groups, such as the Jewish and Greek Orthodox parochial schools. They are the outgrowth in large part, of a strongly felt dissatisfaction with the public schools, not only in terms of their failure to convey the historical substance of the tradition, but also because they have become training houses for secularist values. Their present totalitarian exclusion of religious values, history, and tradition has made necessary the development of alternative educational systems in order to maintain precisely the diversity of cultures and values in our society.

The controversies over *public funding* of private education and the issue of *sex education* in public schools can be argued in many different ways. The fundamental issue, however, is whether the secularist, anti-religious values and libertarian sexual ethics dominant in government-sponsored schools ought to be the exclusive modes of education in a pluralistic society. If the answer is yes, then one asks how the American system differs from the totalitarian systems in the former East bloc, as regards these issues? Alternative education is offered in many culturally homogeneous nations for their minorities, as signs of respect for their identity and integrity. Thus, in Greece, public monies are expended for the tiny Muslim community's educational system, primarily in Thrace. In Finland, a predominantly Lutheran country, public monies are expended to provide for the theological education of future Orthodox priests, *precisely* because they are part of a tiny minority. Canada supports parochial education in numerous ways with state funding for the sake of acknowledging the right of its minorities to be sustained in a culturally plural society. Is this also, a way for the United States to go? Certainly, it is a controversial question. But for the sake of the two-fold goal of education and for the sake of the principle of freedom of religion, it may be the only just way to go.

DILEMMA II: PERSONAL RIGHTS/ PUBLIC REQUIREMENTS IN COMMUNITY

The nature of "community" implies communion of persons, with a measure of shared values, and some sort of a common identity. Until some measure of these things is achieved, there can be no community. On the other side of the equation, however, community does not require a total coincidence of these values and identities. As persons, we are formed in our most intimate communities of families and ethnic, local, and religious traditions. Yet, in the next larger sphere, communities are also places where different groupings of people share values, but in a lesser way and in lesser intensity. Yet, for a community to survive there must be a public morality and a set of public values which provide coherence to these larger, public communities.

The ethical and legal problem arises when values inherent to the individual or smaller communities conflict with those of the larger community. In American history, we have numerous examples of such conflicts. In our history, we have addressed issues of *public decorum and private freedom,* when the ethos of smaller communities conflict with those of the larger community. We do so today, as well. Pluralism in a free society creates this paradox. For example, Mormon polygamy was rejected legally by the larger community in the past.[13] The sale and use of hallucinogenic drugs by private citizens has been prohibited by the laws of the land, just recently even including those drugs traditionally employed by native Americans in religious rites, in a recent Supreme Court decision, *Oregon v. Smith.* Some have seen this act as a providing potential constitutional control of the state over specific religious practices.[14] One spokesman warned "that the opinion was written so broadly that churches could be forced to hire homosexual pastors in cities that have gay-rights laws, and a Catholic church could be forced to hire women as priests, since laws against sex discrimination in employment are 'general law' that apply to everyone." Another commentator, John W. Whitehead, said that the Oregon ruling "alters at least three decades of constitutional jurisprudence involving the free exercise clause and could cause serious harm to minority rights."[15] Similarly, in Boston, a Christian Science couple was tried for treating their ill child with prayer rather than by conventional medicine, because the child died of an allegedly surgically correctable condition. On the other hand, the Supreme Court has quietly ended a nine-year challenge to the tax-exempt status of the Catholic Church for its anti-abortion political activities, but only by means of declaring that those who brought the suit did not have the legal standing to do so.[16]

Here is the paradox: the conflict between public communal ethics as embodied in positive law on the one hand, contrasted by the communal ethics of the personal sphere and in smaller communities, on the other, must co-exist. Pushed to one extreme it will lead to communal inter-fighting such as is taking place in Northern Ireland, Israel/Palestine, and Cyprus. The tactics of the "Rescue Organization" regarding the blocking of abortion clinics is a domestic example. Pushed to the other extreme, conformity to majority positions means the elimination of minority existence. The paradox is that majority sensibilities must include sensitivity for minority rights. Religious rights, first and foremost, need to be protected, not only in terms of their exercise, but also in terms of the overwhelming dominance of majority values, which in essence make minority existence problematical. Clearly, in a sharply pluralistic society, discernment and concern for human integrity is an essential key to addressing the issue.

It may be that all parties involved have to step back from seeking to make certain things legal and illegal so that different communities may co-exist, though there are, of course, limits to what ought to be tolerated in a well-run community. For the Church, it clearly means that we are now more than ever returned to a pre-Constantinian condition, and that communities in conflict ought not to be approached in absolutist terms. As we have seen, majorities fluctuate. In this paradox, regardless of what majorities may say, in either direction, community integrity is critical. It should be a high priority that very few things in the public or legal sphere undermine that integrity. Nevertheless, if it is true that certain behaviors are inimical to community itself (I speak here of the moral content of the Decalogue), then those who see this are required to speak openly and to work forcefully in defense of those moral principles and seek to become the majority. What goes beyond this basic morality can be legislated only if there is sufficient web of consensus to sustain it.[17]

DILEMMA III: DESTRUCTIVE INDIVIDUALISM AND COMMUNITY

This perspective becomes all the more sharply focused when some, or the majorities, or those in power, perceive some behaviors as destructive, not only of individual lives, but of the future generations and of community itself. In principle it is easy to answer the question. If some behaviors are understood as essentially harmful and destructive to both community and personal existence, then the exercise of these acts should be criticized, condemned, and legally, proscribed. It becomes a case of survival for the community. The paradoxical factor, of course, related to this issue is the determination of what, in fact, is destructive to the life of the community and what is entitled to be exercised simply as a personal choice, even though it be perceived as destructive. That the answer is not easy is clear when we examine three current topics of concern: *substance abuse, alcoholism,* and the *sexual revolution.* Our society is handling these in significantly different ways. In regard to substance abuse, the previously mentioned *Oregon v. Smith* case, which prohibited the use of peyote in native American religious rites, clearly expresses the view that substance abuse is of such destructive and negative impact on community life that it must be proscribed, even to the point of limiting religious liberty.

The issue of alcoholism shows a quite different assessment, especially when examined over a period of seventy years or so. The Eighteenth Amendment to the Constitution, passed in 1920, and the Volstead Act, which provided legal guidelines for the prohibition of alcohol use, showed two things. First, that alcohol was perceived by a significant and influential portion of the population as an evil in itself. Secondly, however, this effort showed the impossibility of enforcing a practice without a wide enough web of agreement in the society. In 1933, the Twenty-First Amendment abolished the Eighteenth Amendment.

Within the last few decades, the understanding of the abuse of alcohol has come to take on many meanings. Thus, in the words of one authority, "In the United States, alcoholism may be viewed as a disease, a drug addiction, a learned response to crisis, a symptom of an underlying psychological or physical disorder or a combination of these factors."[18]

The point is that consensus does not exist for this behavioral condition to be addressed by law today. Seventy years ago, anything related to alcohol was deemed to be evil by an element of the society significantly large and influential enough to cause an Amendment to the Constitution to be enacted. The dominant view in public policy today is that alcoholism is an illness, while overt behaviors connected with over-indulgence which harm others, such as drunken driving, are punished by law. This has been increasingly the case since public interest groups such as Mothers Against Drunk Drivers (MADD) and Students Against Drunk Drivers (SADD) have lobbied for stricter enforcement.

The sexual revolution perhaps most clearly shows how the community standards have changed to the point where Christian values regarding pre-marital chastity, adultery, homosexuality, the public exposure of the body, censorship of sexually explicit material, and other such attitudes have essentially been pushed out of public consciousness. Even the thought that these behaviors could be subject to legislation is inconceivable to many today. Conservative Christians abhor the license and degradation. But, as Bellah has shown in *Habits of the Heart*,[19] the combination of Freudianism and the justifications it has given for the expression of human lust, is at present an insurmountable reality in American public life.

What then do smaller communities do in such cases, when they face such disparate situations? The Orthodox have simply sought to affirm their positions, in the first case for the sake of their own members, and in public and practical ways to influence the ethos of society as a whole to direct it as much possible in what it considers a "right direction." In the case of drug and alcohol abuse, for example, the Orthodox Church has expressed it views officially. For example, the Greek Orthodox Archdiocese, at its Clergy-Laity Congresses in 1966, 1970, 1976, and 1978 and subsequently in other ways, has addressed the evils of alcohol and drug abuse. Similarly, it has repeatedly addressed the moral disintegration and secularism of our society, as well as issues of family life, pornography, homosexuality, abortion, and the influence of the mass media.[20] The community cannot enforce issues such as these in the public sphere, unless it is also able to create an ethos in support of its moral stance. *That is why, in the last analysis, these questions are more issues of faith and spiritual commitment than they are issues of legal enforcement.* Thus, while this analysis appears to speak about public issues, at heart it deals with attitudes and stances that need to be cultivated within communities. In this case, the Orthodox Christian ecclesial community.

DILEMMA IV: THOSE WHO SUFFER: EXCLUDED FROM COMMUNITY?

By now, the pattern of approach to these issues of the ethics of community must be clear. In many cases, the Church's teaching, as one of the communities which makes up the larger social fabric, will be at variance. This discontinuity will be either with its society's dominant articulate stance, or more often, the Church will be at variance with the larger community's practices which are not in harmony with its publicly articulated stances.

This is clearly seen in the paradoxical situation of issues such as *hunger, homelessness, and child and spouse abuse.* Here are cases where the smaller communities and the larger community can join together in affirming the same values. What community of Christians, for example, remains unmoved by those who experience hunger, or the homeless, or the abuse of children, or wife-beating? A simple reference to Matthew 25 is sufficient text to undergird such ethical concerns. On the other hand, what politician can rejoice in these same conditions, or advocate ignoring them and hope to be re-elected?

Yet, the last decade has seen a massive government retreat from such concerns in the name of free enterprise. The private sector including the local community in general, and the Churches as well, were supposed to pick up the slack. That they have not done so is clear. The well-being of our communities suffers as a result. We speak one thing and do another. Two thousand years ago, Christ had a name for such behavior.

The answer which comes is dual in character. It means, on

the one hand, focusing more attention to these unacceptable realities in the midst of our communities by the communities themselves in inter-personal ways of acting and through local initiatives. This is what President Bush liked to call "a thousand points of light." But it also means that the larger communities, and the nation as a whole, cannot simply ignore these and other similar issues, if the well-being of the local community and the larger community is to be addressed.

Orthodox ethics would prefer to see programs which enable people to become self-sustaining, to receive help in realizing some of the potentials of community in interpersonal communion, as compared to mere hand-outs. As well, though, a compassionate society must undertake permanent care for those who cannot care for themselves. The assistance and rehabilitative approach better fits the model of growth in the image of God, so appreciated in the Orthodox ethos. It also is supported in the affirmation of Orthodox Christianity for the maintenance of order and mutuality in society than does a predominantly economic *laissez faire* ethic. On this issue, the Fathers of the Church in both East and West have spoken out repeatedly in their concern for the poor and those who suffer deprivation unjustly.[21]

DILEMMA V: VIOLATORS OF COMMUNITY

A similar attitude comes to the fore in Orthodox ethics when it addresses the issue of crime and the issues related with *private and organized lawlessness, criminal justice, the purpose imprisonment, and the death penalty.* In my book, *Contemporary Moral Issues Facing the Orthodox Christian*,[22] I deal with the paradoxes contained in these issues. In a chapter dealing with criminal justice, I note that American law seems to present us with several conflicting purposes for our criminal justice system. In a section titled "Criminal Justice," the question of the purpose of the criminal justice system is addressed in this passage:

> In the public debate, the purpose of our criminal justice system is at question. Some believe that the purpose is retribution – that those who do harm to others should

suffer equivalently. Others hold that the purpose is protection of the innocent and law-abiding public from criminal actions by assuring public order. Still others hold that
the chief purpose is to reform the criminal. Some are very
concerned that the criminal justice system not be used to
suppress minorities and ride roughshod over the rights of
those accused of crimes. At heart, it is hoped that the criminal justice system will deter crime.[23]

The article proposes that none of these views is exclusively
correct, and that the search for a single purpose for the criminal
justice system is erroneous. Each of the purposes mentioned
above is of value for different persons and different situations
and that they are not mutually exclusive.

My conclusion is that even a good criminal justice system is
incapable of solving the question of crime. Persons, rooted in a
world view which affirms the transcendent goodness of God
and the need for human beings to conform to that goodness,
and realizing in sufficient measure the image of God in each of
us, can substantially address the issue of crime. Well-formed
character provides the only effective means to reduce criminal-
ity on the community level. Certainly, communities where human dignity is respected, where good character is prized, and
where mutual interdependence are daily aspects of each person's
experience are profoundly useful. "Yet even this will not suffice
without firm grounding of families and persons in the source of
all law, justice, truth and goodness – God."[24]

In regard to capital punishment, the Orthodox do not always speak with the same voice. In my view, it cannot be ruled
out, even in a well-run society. But, given the capriciousness of
its application in the United States, at least one Orthodox juris-
diction in the United States has come out against it.[25]

DILEMMA VI: CONTEXTS OF COMMUNITY

The environments in which we live are contexts for our communities. To this point, this essay has addressed the social, moral,

and spiritual environments in which communities function. Here the issue is in reference to the physical environments in which people in community live. The topics here are such things as *ecologies, urban design, architecture, and transportation.* Early Christianity by the third or fourth century had displayed its sensitivity to the physical environment for its worship by constructing buildings specifically designed to meet its liturgical needs. In the East, with a few exceptions, churches were built not in grand dimensions, but relatively small and intimate so that the human perspective was not lost in the focus on divine transcendence.[26] Such sensitivity for human living in general was also expressed by Orthodox ethicist Panagiotes Demetropoulos, when he insisted over three decades ago that people have the right to housing which is "well-ventilated, well-illumined, and comfortable."[27]

In short, there is a sense in Orthodox Christianity that housing should enhance human living, but not overwhelm it. What happens to human community in those huge housing projects which destroyed the sense of inter-relatedness and the sense of human proportion? Our post-World War II experiments in such massive, impersonal construction are too well-known for comment.

What should be said about the pollution and destruction of the natural environment out of an Eastern Orthodox perspective? The sacramental approach to the creation, which Orthodox Christianity has consistently expressed, has been at variance with the technological and industrial ravishing of the environment. At an Orthodox Consultation on "Perspectives on Creation" held in 1987 in Sofia, Bulgaria, a remarkable Orthodox ecological document was produced. It was theologically grounded in the Orthodox principles of creation, sacramentality, and human nature, and presented an ecological perspective which has won wide acknowledgement in ecumenical circles. It presents human beings as "priests of Creation," whose task it is to offer the creation back to God eucharistically. Such a perspective cannot justify the created world's exploitation and destruction. For humanity to exercise its ecological priestly function, "dominion" can never be understood as the despoiling of creation. Rather, it must be understood as its care and protection and its use for purposes approved of God.[28]

DILEMMA VII: THE ETHICS OF SUB-COMMUNITIES

There is a sense in which, in America, there are only sub-communities, that is there is no real majority community in our society. We are all minorities in one sense or another. One of the consequences of this reality is the development of sub-community ethics codes, in the form of *professional ethics, industry-wide ethics, and various corporate ethical codes.* This essay cannot deal with these at any length here, but something that the Orthodox ethical mind-set sees, when reading such codes of professional ethics, should be noted. By and large, they are legal documents. They have moved further and further away from the character of those who are to be governed by them and more to conformity with external standards. From an Orthodox ethical perspective, these are disquieting trends.[29] From the perspective of human community, patterned after the community of the relationship of the persons of the Holy Trinity, such an objective, heteronomous, external approach is far from satisfactory. It invites manipulation, rather than genuine caring for the well-being of others. Communities which are held together only by rules, and not by an identity of being and shared loyalties, are in danger for their survival. We have seen in our own days what has happened to several of our most prestigious professions as they have become caught in their commercialization, rather than their identities as privileged members of society because of the service which they offer to others. I speak primarily of the medical and legal professions. Once again, individualism and selfish interest exercise their corrosive influence.

DILEMMA VIII: HEALING COMMUNITY

In Orthodox Christianity today, there is a significant divergence of perspective regarding how the Orthodox ought to relate to the larger society and to communities which are not identical with our interests and values. In the ecumenical field, the dominant view has been a cooperative one where the integrity of the faith permits and the maintenance of a clear demarcation, where it does not. As a result, canonical Orthodoxy has been involved in the ecumenical movement from its earliest days. This does not mean that all Orthodox are comfortable with such involvement, and some Orthodox Churches have not always participated, and some uncanonical Orthodox Churches still do not.

A similar pattern is to be seen among those who write on ethical topics, especially in regard to how the Orthodox ought to relate with the larger community and culture in general. Some hold that Orthodoxy is so discontinuous with the rest of the world, that it is a "city unto itself," a position espoused, for example, by Fr. Michael Azkoul in a strongly "other-worldly" approach. Armenian Orthodox ethicist Vigen Guroian develops a "Detached/Critical" approach, which while not so discontinuous, sees the role of the Orthodox community as one which should refuse to engage with the larger community except to stand in prophetic judgment of it. In a contrary position, Metropolitan George Khodre of Lebanon espouses an incarnationally based "Universalist" approach to other communities and to culture and society in general.

My own view on the subject, which could be labeled an "Integrative/Wholistic" approach, accesses the issue by affirming a paradoxical acceptance of these three views in a complex, reflective mode. Rather than exclude any of these three perspectives, it is better to search out the Christian truth which each seeks to embody. In a comprehensive way, this needs to be done while limiting conclusions drawn from each of them which would tend to *absolutize* their impact upon the Orthodox relationship to culture and other communities.

I am convinced that the Orthodox experience of the relationship of the Faith to culture and of the Church to the world and other communities in them cannot choose among these apparently conflicting views. Each of these affirms at least one major aspect of the Christian faith and the Church as they relate to culture and the world. There are dimensions of Orthodox existence in relationship to other communities, which simply must be rejected and condemned. An almost universal Orthodox example of this is the condemnation of abortion. The line is drawn sharply on this issue.

But unfortunately, it is unquestionably true that historically the Orthodox have often been too accommodating of moral failures around and among them; such failures must be noted and castigated. The prophetic dimension is as essential as outreach for reform is essential. However, the incarnational aspects of the Orthodox Christian Faith do not allow a total disengagement from societies in which we live or only critique and condemnation in relationship to evil among ourselves or in other communities.

The culture-creating traditions of Orthodoxy must also be affirmed. Discernment is needed, and, of course, the perils are many. But all must be held together, if faithfulness to the whole of the scriptural and patristic tradition of faith is to be maintained.[30]

CONCLUSION

In "The Grand Inquisitor" chapter of Dostoevsky's *The Brothers Karamazov*, Christ returns to earth during the Spanish Inquisition and is informed that "nothing has ever been more insupportable for a man and a human society than freedom." There is another value, which is just as difficult for human beings in their fallenness to realize, and that is love.

Little has been said about either freedom or love in the preceding, but for Orthodox Christianity, these two are at the heart of community, for they are at the heart of the Christian ethic. Both freedom and love are nurtured by a reality which transcends the this-worldly values we have been speaking about here. That is why our concerns with community in the world have to be seen always as poor reflections of the life of freedom and love in the Holy Trinity which is present at the heart of the Church's ethic. For that reality to be genuinely experienced, the community of faith in Jesus Christ is essential.

Once that is realized – even in part – the Orthodox can hold that much which expresses the life of divine community can be affirmed in the partial and limited communities which make up our empirically broken human existence.

Orthodox Christians, in considering the life of their ecclesial and parish existence, inevitably are conditioned by the communities of the larger society. How they respond to those communities is conditioned, on the one hand, on how they see themselves. But conversely, how they view those larger communities also conditions how they understand themselves. None of this is simple or subject to an uncontroverted formula. As Orthodox Christians seek to identify with all that is good in the larger communities in which they find themselves, they will recognize in the polarities discussed in this paper both opportunity and danger for the life of their own ecclesial communities and their parish existence. The root of the solution is to be found in their identity as the "people of God," His Church, the "Body of Christ." Do we close ourselves away from the larger communities in which we live? Do we identify with them? Or do we maintain Orthodox Christian integrity as we seek to engage the various expressions of community life in the times and places in which we live? This paper opts for the latter alternative.

I conclude with what I consider to be an eminently inclusive Christian statement that is focused on Jesus Christ that this presentation has served to elaborate. It is from the first chapter of the Epistle to the Colossians:

> (Jesus Christ) is the image of the invisible God, the first-born of all creation; for in him all things were created, in heaven and on earth, visible and invisible, whether thrones or dominions or principalities or authorities – all things were created through him and for him. He is before all things, and in him all things hold together. He is the head

of the body, the church; he is the beginning, the first-born from the dead, that in everything he might be pre-eminent. For in him all the fullness of God was pleased to dwell, and through him to reconcile to himself all things, whether on earth or in heaven.[31]

ENDNOTES

* This paper was presented at the "Ethics: Rights, Responsibilities and Renewal Conference" held at Biola University in La Mirada, CA, June 17-20, 1990.

[1]The topic "Eastern Orthodox Community Ethics" was assigned to me by the organizers of the conference. The meeting was difficult because the Faculty of this conservative Evangelical School voted to abstain from participating in the conference. Only those involved in organizing the conference were in attendance. This led to a strained atmosphere that impacted qualitatively on the presentations and the discussions.

[2]New York: Simon and Schuster, 1987.

[3]All biblical quotations are from the RSV, unless otherwise noted.

[4]"The Small Satanic Worlds of John Calhoun," *Smithsonian*, April, 1970. p. 69ff.

[5]Quoted by David Miller, president and chief executive officer of the J.C. Penney, Co. Commencement address at the University of Missouri, St. Louis, May 10, 1987.

[6]See chapter three of my book, *Toward Transfigured Life: The Theoria of Eastern Orthodox Ethics*. Minneapolis: Light & Life Publ. Co., 1983, especially pp. 59-65 for an ethical critique of existentialism and existentialist ethics in particular.

[7]From David Miller, op. cit.

[8] "But when the Counselor comes, whom I shall send to you from the Father, even the Spirit of truth, who proceeds from the Father, he will bear witness to me."

[9]See Harakas, *Toward Transfigured Life*, chapter six, "The Natural Moral Law." See also, "The Natural Law Teaching of the Eastern Orthodox Church," *The Greek Orthodox Theological Review*. Vol. IX: 2, (1963-1964), pp. 215-224. Reprinted *in New Theology*, No. 2, ed. Martin E. Marty and Dean G. Peerman (New York: The Macmillan

Co., 1965), pp. 122-133.

[10]For my understanding of the general approach of Orthodox Christian Ethics to social concerns as a balanced, coherent, yet paradoxical format, see the following articles: Harakas, "The Church and the Secular World," *Greek Orthodox Theological Review.* Vol. XVII, Spring, (1972), No. 1; "Greek Orthodox Ethics and Western Ethics," *Journal of Ecumenical Studies.* Vol. 10, No. 4, Fall, (1973), pp. 728-751.

[11]Albert Siegel, *Stanford Observer*, as quoted in *The Wittenberg Door.* San Diego, Calif.: Youth Specialities, n.d., p. 68.

[12]R.P.C. Hanson "The Age of the Fathers: Its Significance and Limits" *Eastern Churches Review* 27, 1968), pp. 136.

[13]Reynolds v. United States. 98 U.S. 145, 25 L. Ed. 244 (1878). For the text, consult John J. McGrath, Ed., *Church and State in American Law: Cases and Materials.* Milwaukee: The Bruce Publishing Co., 1962, p. 317 ff.

[14] "Evangelicals express alarm at court's ruling in peyote case," *Religious News Service: Daily News Reports*, May 7, 1990. "In the 6-3 ruling in the case, known as *Oregon v. Smith,* the high court said that a test of 'compelling state interest' need not be applied to most cases involving free exercise of religion. That test was set forth by the Supreme Court in 1963, but the recent ruling said the standard does not outweigh the right of states to bar the use of drugs in religious rituals," p. 8.

[15]Ibid.

[16]*Religious News Service: Daily News Reports*, May 1, 1990, pp. 2-3.

[17]Orthodox ethicist Vigen Guroian, in his book *Incarnate Love: Essays In Orthodox Ethics*, Notre Dame: University of Notre Dame Press, 1988, believes that the Church should stand primarily as a prophetic critic in an essentially non-Christian society. It would seem from this that the Church has no obligation or responsibility to seek to address its moral life or problems, as if from within. I believe that this is not reflective of the tradition of the Orthodox Church through the centuries. Addressing human problems and questions of justice not only by means of critique, but also by positive involvement in public life and the legislative process, is one aspect of the "outreach" dimension of the Church's existence, a part of its "catholic" dimension. In later publications, it seems that Prof. Guroian has modified this position so that it allows for more involvement of the Orthodox Christian in what is called in this paper the "communities" in which Orthodox

Christianity finds itself located in time and space.

[18]The *New Encyclopaedia Britannica: Micropaedia, Fifteenth Ed*. Chicago: Encyclopaedia Britannica, 1985, vol. 1, p. 228.

[19]Robert N. Bellah, et. al., *Habits of the Heart: Individualism and Commitment in American Life*. New York: Harper and Row, 1985.

[20]For texts and a history of this involvement regarding the Orthodox Church, and in particular the Greek Orthodox Archdiocese, see Stanley S. Harakas*, Let Mercy Abound: Social Concern in the Greek Orthodox Church*. Brookline, MA: Holy Cross Orthodox Press, 1983. For an outline of Clergy-Laity Congress actions on social and moral issues, see pp. 107-109.

[21]For a good survey of this patristic concern for the poor and the unjustly treated see Peter C. Phan, *Social Thought. Message of the Fathers of the Church*, vol. 20. Wilmington, DL: Michael Glazier, 1984.

[22]Minneapolis: Light and Life Publishing Co., 1982.

[23]Ibid., p. 151.

[24]Ibid., p. 154.

[25]See section 39 of *Contemporary Moral Issues Facing the Orthodox Christian*, op. cit., p. 154 ff.

[26]John Yiannias, "Orthodox Art and Architecture," in *A Companion to the Greek Orthodox Church*, ed. Fotios K. Litsas, New York: Department of Communication - Greek Orthodox Archdiocese, 1984, p. 91ff.

[27]Panagiotes Ch. Demetropoulos, Ὀρθόδοξος Χριστιανικὴ Ἠθικὴ (Orthodox Christian Ethics). Athens, 1970, p. 161.

[28]See the Sofia Report "Orthodox Perspectives on Creation" in *Justice, Peace and the Integrity of Creation: Insights from Orthodoxy*. Ed. Gennadios Limouris. Geneva: WCC Publications, 1990, pp. 1-15.

[29]For an interesting Roman Catholic approach to the issue of professional ethics, see William F. May, "The Virtues in a Professional Setting," *The Annual of the Society of Christian Ethics: 1984*. Ed., Larry L. Rasmussen. Vancouver, B.C.: The Society of Christian Ethics, 1984, 71-91.

[30]For some of my views on this issue, more fully articulated, see my article "Orthodoxy in America: Continuity, Discontinuity, Newness," in *Orthodox Perspectives on Pastoral* Praxis. Ed. Theodore Stylianopoulos. Brookline, MA: Holy Cross Orthodox Press, 1988, pp. 13-29, as well as other articles to be found in the footnotes.

[31]Colossians 1.15-20.

.